The Fittest Food Lovers

Lovers

How EVERY BODY Can be Incredibly Fit *and* Still Enjoy Food

Josh,
Enjoy fellow sports &
food lover ♡

Cheers,
Kristina

KRISTINA V. REYNOLDS

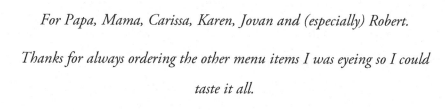

For Papa, Mama, Carissa, Karen, Jovan and (especially) Robert.

Thanks for always ordering the other menu items I was eyeing so I could taste it all.

Kristina Villanueva Reynolds is a life-long food lover and athlete. Born in the Midwest and raised in the San Francisco Bay Area, she was exposed to a wide variety of cuisines—all of which she acquired a taste for. Additionally, she has always been a natural competitor, winning team and individual accolades in every sport she participated in since grade school. Unfortunately, due to a serious injury in her late teens, she was unable to continue participating in organized sports. However, her competitive nature and love for sports never waned. She has maintained a very active and healthy food-filled lifestyle over the years.

Kristina currently resides in San Diego, CA. She enjoys traveling to experience authentic cuisines from different countries and regions while engaging in a multitude of activities including, but not limited to: golf, basketball, tennis, indoor rock climbing, hiking, kayaking, paddle boarding, skiing, snowboarding, snorkeling and swimming. She holds a B.S. in Management Science from the University of California, San Diego and is the Founder & CEO of Glutto Inc.

Table of Contents

Introduction

What is the purpose of this book?

The Fittest Food Lovers is a source of information and inspiration for anyone who wants to improve their fitness while building a healthy relationship with food. Contrary to popular belief, being fit and loving food are not mutually exclusive. In fact, these are two of the best things you can do for your body. Food is necessary to live, so why not enjoy it? Exercise is vitally important as well, so why not enjoy that too? Finding ways to make the necessary things in life fun and enjoyable makes them sustainable, reduces stress and increases happiness—which is a primary contributor to a healthy life too.

As you may know, there is not one bulletproof method of eating and working out that will yield the absolute best results for everyone because every single body is different. This book covers those with a wide range of body types and ethnic backgrounds, so certain featured individuals may naturally be more relatable to different people. You can read about what has decidedly worked for specific types of people and you may have the best success emulating those whom you relate to the most.

Some of you might be questioning, "What do I have in common with these world-class athletes and public figures? I'm not sure I can relate to any of them." Well, don't be so quick to judge. Maybe you have similar taste preferences as someone in this book and can learn about healthier dining alternatives that you may not have known about. Perhaps you may come across a method of eating that works well with your lifestyle or simply piques your interest. Or, maybe someone you didn't initially relate to opens your eyes to a type of physical activity that you find interesting and it ends up becoming part of your regular workout routine. Also, consider a scenario in which you're looking to build your wealth. Would you want to learn the mindset and tactics of a successful billionaire (someone who doesn't closely resemble your current situation), or someone making a slightly-above-average income (someone who more closely resembles your current situation)? Don't sell yourself short. You deserve to learn from the best.

You can gain new perspectives. Or, you may find helpful nuggets of information from multiple people that you can apply to your life. The insights and tips dispensed in this book are not "one-size-fits-all," so read through it to discover what is most effective for you.

We've included the knowledge and wisdom of top certified professionals in the nutrition and fitness worlds. These experts help dispel any sort of misinformation about food and fitness proliferated in the media and on the internet.

This book was also written to help fight world hunger. We released the initial version of this book on Thanksgiving 2019, the biggest holiday in the United States revolving around food and gratitude. A portion of the proceeds of each new book purchased will be donated to select charitable organizations dedicated to fighting hunger.

Note: *The majority of the content in this book came from 1-on-1 interviews between the featured individuals and the author, Kristina V. Reynolds. The language used by each person is kept as accurate as possible, whether or not it is grammatically correct. (So put away your whistles and relax, grammar police.)*

What are the qualifications to become one of "the fittest food lovers?"

First of all, let's break down the terms "fittest" and "food lover."

The "fittest" refers to those in the highest levels of physical health and condition for their respective fields. They are functionally fit, not just aesthetically fit. In other words, these people can physically perform at elite levels in their professional fields and don't simply look the part. For example, bodybuilders may portray the image of Greek gods with their chiseled muscular physiques, but because they primarily train for aesthetics, some of these competitors encounter major side effects that negatively impact their health physically and psychologically. Other athletes or performers may purge their bodies of essential liquids or nutrients to get that "perfect" look. Looking extremely fit doesn't always equate to being healthy and vice versa. Those who are considered to be "the fittest" are healthy inside and out.

"Food lover" is an all-encompassing term for food enthusiasts of all types. (I broke down the meaning of food lovers, foodies and everything in between in an article for my company blog, Glutto Digest, called "Foodies vs. Food Lovers - What's the Difference?" Google it.) If you're asking, "Well, isn't everyone a food lover?" Frankly, the answer is "no." Not everyone finds joy in food and eating. Some people see food as mere fuel and force themselves to eat only what they think will benefit their bodies. Others who may appear to enjoy food have an unhealthy obsession leading to excessive weight gain and other health issues. Some have other eating disorders and have not yet found a method to enjoy food while maintaining a healthy body and mind. Those who are featured in this book have not lost that joy and have learned to embrace their love for food in a healthy manner.

When my team and I selected the individuals for this book, we wanted to provide a solid representation of people from distinct backgrounds who have: 1) shown a great appreciation for food and 2) are well-known for maintaining an elite level of physical fitness. When it comes to enjoying food and staying fit, these people have figured out what works best for them.

Whether or not an individual meets these qualifications is subjective since it is highly implausible to get access to medical records and vital signs of everyone nominated to objectively select candidates. Also, no specific body type was required to meet the aforementioned criteria, just a superior level of overall health and physical capabilities. Everyone has different bodies and each person's physical appearance is different at their peak levels of health...You wouldn't expect a world champion weightlifter to have the same body type as an Olympic gold medalist figure skater, would you? Yet, the fitness levels of both these individuals would be off the charts.

Admittedly, with the billions of people that populate this planet, there are theoretically thousands of people who deserve to be featured in this book. However, it's logistically impossible to find and coordinate with every single one of them given finite time and resources. We are immensely grateful for every single person featured in the forthcoming pages and thank them for their generosity of time and dispensing of valuable information.

Disclosure: The content in this book includes information, advice and guidance related to healthcare. It is intended to act as a supplement to the advice of your healthcare professional. Please consult a medical professional before making any changes to your nutrition, fitness or health. The author and publisher of this book disclaim liability for any medically-related results that may occur following the application of any information, advice or guidance contained in this book.

REASON

A nostalgic scent permeates the air, delighting my olfactory nerves while awakening the monster in my stomach from its temporary slumber. The Pied Piper-like allure of this far-reaching aroma coaxes bystanders to join an ever-growing line. As I approach the origin of this invisible ambrosial charmer, a welcome sight greets me: a proud army of cinnamon rolls, glistening beneath a translucent white glaze.

I must have one.

Although the line at the booth appears to be a reasonable length, the wait is nearly unbearable. My stomach monster growls with impatience. Ten minutes feels like an hour and my borborygmus grows increasingly audible. After what seems like a lifetime, I finally reach the front of the line and get my hands on one of those hot, gooey rolls. When I sink my teeth into the soft and chewy treat, my overstimulated salivary glands gush uncontrollably. Every morsel releases a burst of delectable sweet cinnamon filling, smothering my yearning taste buds. As my satiated stomach monster returns to sleep, I hear Louis Armstrong singing in his rich gravelly baritone, "Heaven. I'm in heaven."

I could wax poetic about food all day. (I attribute much of my occasional magniloquence and syntactic structure, i.e., "artsy-fartsy language," to spending my adolescence soaking up the speech of the articulate characters of *Dawson's Creek* and *10 Things I Hate About You*, and even the *Bring It On* cheerleader who constantly spewed out esoteric SAT words.) I love the flavors, the textures, the smells, the sights and sounds—not to mention the accompanying camaraderie, experiences and memories. Food, when done right, is an experiential work of art that invigorates all the human senses, and these lip-smacking cinnamon rolls certainly pass the test.

As I enjoy my sugary midday delight, an elderly stranger asks me something I've been asked countless times, "So, where does it all go?"

Her question yanks me out of my dream-like state. I recognize she means this rhetorical question as a compliment, given my lean figure, so I make a small joke about feeding my pet tapeworm and the stranger chuckles in content.

However, this harmless interaction sparks a memory of being asked the same question in my early 20s in an unexpectedly serious and slightly accusatory tone, as if I were cheating the system. The exact scenario evades me, but the emotions remain clear. The woman who questioned my eating exhibited signs of jealousy, frustration and despair. Our short chat revealed that she had been struggling with food and weight issues. I felt awful at the time that I didn't know how to properly respond to her. I had never really given my eating habits much thought. For the first couple decades of my life, I simply ate whatever food was in front of me.

I was raised in a small suburban city called Belmont, located on the Peninsula in the San Francisco Bay Area, in a Filipino-American household. If you know anything about Filipinos, you know that they love, *love*, *LOVE* their food, from *adobo* to *longanisa* to *lumpia* to *turon* to *halo-halo*... I could go on and on. While full of fantastic flavors, most traditional Filipino food isn't exactly the healthiest stuff on earth. Many dishes are packed with saturated fats, sodium or added sugars. Plus, a small mountain of white rice accompanies nearly every meal. Not only did my family and I eat traditional Filipino meals fairly regularly, but like most American families in the late 80s and early 90s, we ate fast food and drank soda all the time. It was convenient and we were relatively ignorant about the dietary repercussions, as was most of society at the time. Although I grew up eating a lot of meals that seem terribly unhealthy in retrospect, I somehow ended up as a perfectly healthy adult.

How was this possible?

It would be logical to assume that my passion for food was in my blood, as perhaps has become evident by now, but that wasn't always the case. My earliest memories of eating date back to when I was a little girl of four or five. My mom always made delicious home-cooked meals for our family. But at that age, eating was more of a chore for me than an enjoyment. It just didn't interest me. My taste buds—and the rest of me—were far from mature, so I couldn't pick up on the beautiful flavor nuances of certain dishes. It all tasted pretty much the same to my puerile palate. All the salty fast food and sugary sodas I consumed probably didn't help. Some nights at the dinner table, I would endlessly pick at my plate of chicken adobo. However, when my dad fed me a spoonful of *his* food, it tasted infinitely better. In fact, it was the same exact chicken adobo, but for some reason, everything tasted better off of my dad's plate.

This was how my love for food began—through a psychological trick.

My adventurousness around food quickly expanded beyond my plate and my dad's. Besides Filipino and American food, we had Italian, Japanese and Thai cuisines on rotation. When my family and I went out to eat, my dad would put samples of different dishes on my plate. He instilled a "don't knock it till you've tried it" attitude about food in me. Out of curiosity, coupled with trust born of the fact that every type of food he had given me in the past tasted good, I always tried the sample dishes. I almost always ended up liking them.

I reveled in eating foods that were out of the ordinary foods for me as a kid, like frog legs—which, by the way, taste like incredibly tender chicken. I also remember my dad telling me to add Tabasco sauce to savory foods like eggs or pasta to make them exciting, thus sparking my foray into spicy foods. Tasting foods and spices I had never tried before was like completing achievements in a video game. If it hadn't been for my dad making food interesting and exciting, I never would have fully realized the joy of eating, nor would I have realized how good my mom's cooking truly was.

I am not a glutton—I am an explorer of food.

-Erma Bombeck

As my palate evolved, so did my appetite. By the time I was 10, eating was no longer a tedious endeavor, but an enjoyable activity. Luckily, I had developed an interest in sports to balance things out. I was athletically gifted and became fully engaged in playing the fall and winter sports that my mom signed me up for at my grade school, volleyball and basketball. I fell in love with playing basketball instantly because my dad had begun taking me to Golden State Warriors games with him back when Chris Mullin was a member of the "Dream Team."

Being physically active every day proved a huge benefit to my overall health. As a natural competitor, I hated to lose as much as I loved to win, so I was always practicing drills and shooting hoops in my backyard. I particularly enjoyed playing one-on-one, HORSE and Around the World. I never worried about what I ate because I was active and slightly underweight. In fact, my parents wanted me to eat more to bulk up and get stronger so I wouldn't get pushed around on the court around by the bigger girls or get injured. I drank Ensure between meals for additional calories and nutrients each day. We even had a second refrigerator in the garage filled with cases of the meal supplement.

At twelve, I could eat a large pizza all by myself within a couple of sittings, yet I still barely met the average weight for a girl my height, approximately 5'4". It may be worth noting that I was eating cheeseless pizzas, which were generally unheard of in the 90s. My dad, an M.D. who was a bit forward-thinking when it came to diet, would order pizzas without cheese. He knew, even before the rest of society caught on, that all that saturated fat would be terrible for my health. Consequently, I avoided most cheeses even though I wasn't lactose intolerant. Also, the oleaginous lumps of cheese that I removed from "normal" pizza slices reminded me of the antagonist of the classic satirical film *Spaceballs*, Pizza the Hutt, whom I found disgusting. If the saying "you are what you eat" was true, the last thing I wanted to be was Pizza the Hutt. Luckily, this aversion didn't extend to the point of *turophobia*, the irrational fear of cheese, because then I would have never developed an appreciation for the artisanal cheeses I love.

Tell me what you eat, and I will tell you what you are.

-Anthelme Brillat-Savarin

In high school, I swapped volleyball for golf but continued playing basketball. I was finally gaining some size and getting stronger and all the accolades that came along with excelling at sports didn't hurt. Motivated and excited about my growth, I played varsity basketball until my junior year.

Then came a freak accident.

It was Cinco de Mayo and I went out to the front lawn with my Spanish class to celebrate. A piñata full of candy hung from a tree. A few students valiantly attempted to hit the piñata blindfolded with a steel baseball bat. You can guess what followed. Evidently, I was laser-focused on grabbing the candy on the ground because I never felt any pain when that metal bat made swift, solid contact with the left side of my cranium. I felt worse for my fellow teenage classmates than I did for myself. They had to witness a crimson fountain spewing from my split scalp onto my now blood-soaked hoodie, which happened to be white for full horrific effect.

I'm incredibly grateful that my skull remained intact and I didn't suffer extensive brain damage. Unfortunately, and most disappointingly, this officially marked the end of my basketball career. The occasional bouts of vertigo, induced by abrupt movements, would persist for years. At least I could still play golf, but that didn't provide the same level of activity as basketball.

I headed south to sunny San Diego to attend the University of California, San Diego (UCSD). Because I had decided not to pursue collegiate-level sports, my regular physical activity decreased drastically. Concurrently, my eating habits deteriorated. Home-cooked meals were no longer readily available, so I resorted to standard dining hall fare and nearby fast food. Trips to Carl's Jr., Jack-in-the-Box, Round Table Pizza and Wendy's were routine. My designated cupboard shelf in the kitchen of my shared apartment was full of chips and sugary snacks. I rarely bought fresh fruits or vegetables because I could never seem to eat them before they rotted or grew moldy.

After a couple of years without regular exercise and deteriorating eating habits, I was about twenty percent heavier than I had been when I played basketball. Although I was technically still within the healthy weight range for a woman my height, it wasn't ideal. I felt sluggish, moody and uncomfortable in my ever-tightening jeans. I was surprisingly oblivious to the fact that my routine was directly affecting my overall well-being.

Weeks after graduating from college, I experienced a major shift in my health when my family and I went on a vacation to the Philippines to visit our relatives.

Remember how Filipinos love their food? Whenever my family and I traveled to the Philippines, we would be greeted with a massive feast— not just for our arrival, but for almost every meal during our stay, including "merienda," which are snacks eaten in between meals. This trip was no different. Filipinos are some of the most hospitable people in the world. They want to make sure their guests are well-fed, especially if they are family. Like many cultures with tight-knit families, in the Filipino culture, food=happiness.

A few days in, I felt like I was in food up to my eyeballs. To get my digestive system back in order, I spent the remaining two weeks of our trip inadvertently fasting in the mornings and eating lighter Filipino foods like *laing* (a spicy vegetable dish), *sinigang na isda* (a savory stew with fresh fish) and *monggo* (a mung bean soup). I literally couldn't stomach anything heavy. In addition to curtailing my eating, I walked beyond the equivalent of a marathon under the hot equatorial sun as we trekked around sightseeing. I was drenched in sweat every day, so I was rehydrating with bottled water nonstop.

When I got back to the states, my friends all noticed something different about me. They remarked that I looked slimmer and lighter (weight-wise, not skin tone-wise—I actually got about five shades darker). My clothes fit better. What was crazy was that this was completely unintentional. No one ever told me I needed to shed pounds, not even my doctors, so I never made a deliberate attempt to do so. Yet, this change made me more energetic, confident and, most importantly, much happier. This was the "me" I had wanted to be.

Some of you may be thinking, "What the heck? You didn't go through any massive transformations. You weren't obese and you didn't have to lose hundreds of pounds. You don't even know what it's like to be really fat or super scrawny!"

All true. While overcoming those extreme hardships is immensely admirable, I cannot personally identify with those struggles. I don't compare myself to the people who face them, although I have learned a lot from the individuals featured in the following chapters who generously shared their wide range of experiences.

So, why share *my* background? Simply put, to illustrate that I'm a devout food lover who has experienced both kinds of challenges around weight. I've been on the smaller side and wanted to put on weight. I've been too big for my frame and wanted to lose weight. But most importantly, I've meticulously dissected and learned from those and the rest of my experiences, evolving to the point that I have been able to effortlessly enjoy whatever food I want while still being perfectly healthy and fit—for more than a decade and counting.

For much of my life, I thought I was immune to all the negative effects of food. I wrongly took pride in not having to exercise every day and in eating anything I desired without becoming excessively heavier. I was in denial that transformations were taking place in my body as a result of the way I ate over time. Not until I looked back on photos of myself years later did I clearly see the positive and negative effects that food and fitness—or the lack thereof—had on me, both physically and emotionally. Had I not changed my ways, I would have remained on a steady path towards self-destruction. I wasn't immune. As it turns out, no one is.

You may be saying, "But I thought you can eat anything and be super fit!" That is correct. To foreshadow what comes in later chapters, time plays a huge role. What, how and when we eat over time matters. Our habits and lifestyles matter. Even those who don't gain weight while constantly eating the unhealthiest of foods are doing damage inside their bodies. These types of people are now commonly known as "skinny fat." If someone like me, who is genetically predisposed to weigh less than average (according to a DNA test I took), can still fall victim to the negative effects of a poor diet, then anyone can be affected.

Each person has their own unique journey and goals, but I hope that sharing my and others' experiences can shed a little light on the best path for you.

Lorena Abreu

Lorena Abreu is a professional parkour athlete. She has been a regular performer in highly regarded shows including Cirque du Soleil and Universal's Islands of Adventure in Orlando. She has also been featured in TKO with Kevin Hart.

FOOD

- Type of eater: Omnivore—I was pescetarian for a couple of years, but I'm someone who does a lot of physical activity and it wasn't working for me. Even though I did eat fish, I did feel much better once I started eating meat and chicken again.
- Adventurous level: 8

- Taste preferences: I like it all: spicy, sweet, savory...not bitter though. I hate coffee and alcohol, so anything bitter I really don't like.
- Ethnicity: Dominican Republic and Lebanese

KVR: Do you attribute any of your taste preferences to your ethnicity, or is there something else that you give credit to for your tastes?

LA: I guess to a certain point your tastes are genetic and hereditary. I remember we did a weird litmus test in high school that tested the number of taste buds that you have, some people have more and some people have less. I and maybe one other person gagged when we tasted this paper and everyone else didn't taste anything. I think that's why I'm averse to bitter.

My mom definitely shaped my culinary preferences. My dad made me a fan of spicy and seafood...and my mom everything else.

KVR: What are some of your favorite cuisines?

LA: I love Japanese cuisine. I love *love* Japanese cuisine and obviously Dominican cuisine.

KVR: Do you follow a certain diet or meal plan? How does it work for you?

LA: Yeah, it's interesting. Last year, I started studying for my personal training certification, so I got more into the fitness world online. I was learning about all these different diets and different ways of eating. Then, I started meticulously calculating my macronutrients: my ratio of carbohydrates to fats to proteins. I literally was calculating everything I ate. It didn't start that way, but it became that way. It's basically an eating disorder once you become so concerned about every single thing you eat. You don't even enjoy food anymore. Friends ask you if you want to eat out and it stresses you out. At that point, when food is controlling you and not the other way around, it's an eating disorder. So I realized I wasn't doing myself any favors and I kinda relaxed and tried to think less about exactly what I was eating and just tried to eat healthily.

As weird as it sounds, I just did a reality show where they controlled our food. It's like survivor meets obstacle course racing called Exatlón. So, I had already begun to break that habit of worrying about my food. This TV show was just the nail in the coffin. Now, I don't let food be stressful for me. I at least try to eat a lot of raw food. I just focus on eating healthy things and give my body what it wants by eating intuitively. Maybe this is getting too personal, but I tend to be on the constipated side...so that's especially why eating a lot of raw food makes me feel good. Outside of that, if I want to have some sweets or something, I let myself have some now and then.

KVR: Can you give me an example of typical dishes you'll have throughout the day for breakfast, lunch and dinner? Any go-to snacks?

LA: Yeah, so right now I'm integrating back into real life. I was completely and absolutely disconnected from real life in a total sequester on the show. What I've been eating once I got out is a couple of eggs and I'm obsessed with cereal. I like to mix two cereals...I can't have just one. I like mixing peanut butter puffs with bran flakes with bits of banana and strawberry. Right now I have a bag of kale in the fridge, which I actually enjoy. I try to eat some raw veggies and raw fruits throughout my day. Everything else just changes on a day-to-day basis. I like to cook a lot of different things.

For snacks, I've been really obsessed with watermelon and cantaloupe since I got out, which are things I didn't like before the reality show. Otherwise, I really like cereal. I'm just obsessed with cereal.

KVR: What are some foods you'd normally avoid, but crave...like cheat-day foods?

LA: Hmm. I don't know. Since I changed my mindset, I do let myself eat stuff like ice cream and pizza. As long as I eat enough of the healthy stuff, I can tell my body's happy. Ahh, I don't even know cause a lot of times, the gross stuff you used to like as a kid doesn't feel good to eat anymore. I just had a bunch of Chips Ahoy cookies the other day and I actually felt gross afterward.

KVR: What are some of your all-time favorite foods?

LA: At Thanksgiving with my family, someone made pastelon de platano maduro, which is like a casserole of sweet plantains with ground beef. That was the entirety of Thanksgiving for me. That was insane.

I love tempura...the way the Japanese fry their food. Anything tempura-fried, any vegetable, any sea creature is just so good.

I'm also kind of a foodie. Before I left for the show, I was visiting New York and I had a bucket list of all the places I wanted to try food at. In the summer, they have all these cool food stands with foods from different countries. I like all kinds of different kinds of foods. That's why it's so hard to tell you what I normally eat because I like to keep it really different.

KVR: What are some of your all-time least favorite foods?

LA: I don't know because everything I didn't like before the show (like corn and melons), I like now. For me, it's more drinks. As much as a coffeeholic my mom is, I still can't bring myself to like coffee. I can't drink any drinks with any bitterness.

Actually, you know what? Any flavorless food. Flavorless food makes me very sad...like when someone just sticks a whole chicken breast in the oven—a dry, non-seasoned chicken breast—and they say that's dinner. It makes me so sad.

KVR: What are some of your favorite restaurants?

LA: I really like the concept of "build-your-own bowl" restaurants. There's a bunch of them in New York and I'm sure they have a bunch of them in most big cities. They have the ingredients laid out in front of you and you pick what you want in your bowl, wrap, or whatever.

KVR: When you go grocery shopping, do you have any favorite foods or beverages that you often get?

LA: Something that I always have, but I order online, is chai tea powder mix. I make my own chai tea lattes with cashew milk. That is one of the things I can't live without.

FITNESS

KVR: How would you describe your natural body type? Are you naturally lean, athletic or curvy?

LA: I don't know what it's like to be not athletic. I'm very lucky that my parents have had me in a lot of sports and have always inspired me to move a lot and do a lot of exercise since I was little. I don't know what my natural body type is because I've never known a life that wasn't athletic. So, I think it's athletic.

Actually, my brother doesn't exercise, but you can tell his body *wants* to be athletic. As soon as he does anything, his shoulders, his back and everything are like "Boom! Boom!"

KVR: As a professional parkour athlete, I'm sure you do a lot of calisthenics. Are there any other go-to exercises or physical activities that you do?

LA: Yeah, beside parkour I really like Olympic weightlifting. That's something I've been learning in the past year. I really, really enjoy that.

I also really like Chinese pole. It's a circus discipline. It's one of the pole arts where the pole is thicker and wrapped in rubber tape and you do bodyweight acrobatics up and down the pole. It's really fun. It's a perfect complement to parkour because it's way more upper body. Being on the pole requires ten things that basically use every muscle in your body, so at all times everything is working. It's a great, great thing to do for a workout.

KVR: So at what point were you happy with your overall fitness?

LA: That's a difficult question cause I think I've spent most of my life not happy like "I can always be better, I can always be better, I can always be better…" It's interesting cause in the past I've not been satisfied with my physical condition. Then months later, I'll look back at videos of myself at that time and be like "Man, I was killing it. What was I worried about?" But then at the present time, it's always that same thing, thinking "I can always be better…" I think, especially from talking to other girls, that's something a lot of us go through. A little bit of that [mindset] is a good thing, but too much of it is definitely a bad thing. For us women in sports and fitness, we need to be kind to ourselves. It's something that I still struggle with, appreciating what you already have and not focusing so much on what you imagine in your mind you could be.

When I became obsessed with being "perfectly healthy," I realized that was abnormal and not fun and not a way for anyone to live their life. That's also when I came to the conclusion about [accepting] my body image. Especially when I started talking to girls on Instagram and other girls in parkour asking me what I eat and telling me their experiences, I realized I was not the only one who was overly concerned with how I looked and how I ate.

You know, I never used to really care much about how I looked. I've been doing ab exercising since high school and always liked having abs, but I never started to look at myself negatively until a couple of years into training parkour when I started getting into personal training as well as the fitness culture online. That's when I started over-analyzing everything about myself. I'd look at all these before & after pictures and compare myself. It's all psychological.

But it's interesting because now there's this counter-culture that's coming out of this, focusing on body positivity and intuitive eating. A lot of people try to market "flexible dieting," which is counting your macronutrients. These people say you can eat all of these different foods as long as it fits your macros, but it's still an eating disorder...It's still being obsessed with what you eat and counting every single thing that you're putting into your body. Intuitive eating is what I'm doing now: just eating things that you already know are good for you and that will nourish you and then just chill out. Also, people are now posting reverse before & after pictures where they were shredded and not necessarily healthy, especially mentally, and an after picture where they look absolutely normal and ten times more happy and healthy overall not killing themselves over food and exercise.

KVR: What keeps you motivated to maintain such a high level of fitness?

LA: It just happens to be what I like to do. I really like to move. Some people like to solve Rubik's cubes, which I will never understand, but some people will never understand why I like to jump on walls. It just happens to be what really, really excites me. Not everyone has a passion for a discipline that physical. The most important thing for everyone is to find some sort of physical activity that they actually enjoy because there are so many options out there. Chances are that there's something that you're gonna find fun.

KVR: So you've been on a wide variety of stages from Universal Orlando's Sinbad and Cirque du Soleil to an episode of Kevin Hart's TKO. Out of all your experiences, which one is your favorite?

LA: Oh man. Well, Exatlón was definitely one of the best and worst things I've ever done. It's definitely one of the most intense things I've done on all fronts. Gosh, I can't pick. Each project is so special in its own way. Each and every one of them is life-changing in the time when it comes.

KVR: Any other tips regarding fitness or eating?

LA: My main tip, especially to women everywhere, is just chill out. Let yourself enjoy food. Find something physical that you actually enjoy...and don't overdo it because then you just ruin exercising for yourself and then you create a negative mental association with exercise. Not everyone has to be a crazy fitness person and definitely not everyone needs crazy abs and glutes. There's nothing wrong with having some fat. There's nothing wrong with enjoying the foods you like. Just try to eat healthy foods and eat raw foods whenever you can. Give your body things to nourish it and enjoy life!

Lizzie Armanto

Lizzie Armanto is a professional skateboarder competing in the Tokyo 2020 Olympics, the inaugural year of skateboarding in the Olympics. She became the first female in history to complete an entire 360° ramp.

FOOD

- Type of eater: Omnivore
- Adventurous level: 8—I like to try new stuff that's out of my comfort zone, but I'm not looking for the most outlandish things.
- Taste preferences: sweet, savory—I really like to mix it up though, so I'm not stuck to one thing.

- Ethnicity: ½ Finnish, ¼ Filipino and the rest is Scottish, Irish and English (My dad is from Finland and I was born in the US, so I have dual citizenship.)

KVR: Do you attribute any of your taste preferences to your ethnicity, or is there something else that you give credit to for your tastes?

LA: I really think my tastes have become the way they are from a mix of it all. Growing up, my mom would make Filipino food for family get-togethers and that's been one of my favorite foods. When I'm at home, I eat a lot of Asian food. When I travel, I try to try stuff from where I'm at.

KVR: What would you say are some of your favorite cuisines?

LA: That's such a tough question. Like I said, I really like Filipino food, but I don't know it as diversely as I know some other cuisines. I do like what I have tried. I also really like Thai food and Japanese food.

I would also be able to pick one type of food over another depending on if I'm eating food in the country that it's from and depending who's making it. You just have to be careful sometimes when you're abroad.

KVR: Do you follow a certain diet or do you pretty much eat what you want?

LA: I'd like to say that I eat whatever I want, but I kinda stay away from fast food because I don't like to feel shitty. When I'm at home, I can regulate what I'm eating better, but on the road, I'm a lot more loose with my diet.

KVR: Can you give me an example of a typical dish you'll have for breakfast, lunch and dinner? Any go-to snacks?

LA: For breakfast, I'm either having oatmeal or eggs and toast. Those are my staples. For lunch, I'll have poke or sushi...It really depends on where I am. Sometimes, I'll make a sandwich at home. Then for dinner, it could be anything depending on where I'm at. Thai food is a go-to. I make fried rice at home sometimes. I'll usually have a boba tea a couple times a week as well.

In the fall, I'll eat apples as a snack because there will be a lot of really good ones out. When I'm in Europe, I'll snack on a bunch of different types of breads. It's always so fresh there.

KVR: Are there some foods that you'll normally avoid, but crave? Any "cheat day" foods?

LA: There are times when I think, "Uh, I really want something sweet." Then I'll have some fruit versus going in on cake or ice cream.

There are also times like when I got back from Europe and I said, "I don't want to eat any more pasta or bread." Not that I was over it, but I needed a break. So, I went back to eating more greens like salads or veggie dishes.

KVR: What are some of your all-time favorite foods?

LA: I love chicken adobo and dumplings...I think they're Taiwanese dumplings. That's all that's coming to mind now, but I know there's other stuff.

KVR: What are some of your all-time least favorite foods?

LA: I'm not a fan of pâté or asparagus. I also don't like anything with organs like liver. I'll try it, but then I'm usually like, "Ok, that's that. I'm good." I avoid escargot as well. Actually, one thing that I was afraid to try was the black fungus in China. It's very pungent. I mean, people eat it and they say it tastes good, but the smell is too strong for me. In my head, it's like putting a dirty foot in your mouth.

KVR: What are some of your favorite restaurants?

LA: There's a place called Homemade Cafe up in the Bay (in Berkeley). It's one of my favorite breakfast restaurants. It kinda feels like a diner and all their food is homemade. Their corned beef hash is out of this world.

My favorite tea house is also in the bay (San Francisco) and it's called Asha Tea House. All their teas are artisan. They'll use purees to flavor their teas instead of syrup. Also, their boba's really good.

So many good places...Koraku in Little Tokyo in LA is really good. Thai One On in Vista is a really good Thai place. There's this vegetarian restaurant called Sipz in San Diego that I like going to that has really good steam buns. They're like BBQ pork buns, but not real pork. I also like Din Tai Fung in Costa Mesa...There's a bunch of them, but that's the one I go to.

KVR: When you go grocery shopping, do you have any favorite foods or beverages you'll usually get?

LA: My grocery shopping is pretty limited because I pretty much only get stuff for breakfast, unless I'm planning on making dinner (which isn't as frequent). I usually get the basics, like eggs and toast. I also get these anti-inflammatory juice shots from Frazier Farms that have turmeric, lemon, ginger, pineapple...and it's really refreshing. I'll have that every morning when I wake up.

KVR: Do you plan on adjusting what you eat as you prepare for the Olympics?

LA: I like to just go off of how my body's doing and adjust what I eat as needed. If I get an injury, I'll go on an anti-inflammatory diet.

FITNESS

KVR: How do you describe your natural body type? Lean, athletic, or curvy?

LA: I'm on the leaner side. When I was growing up, I was tall and lanky, but now I'm more proportionate. When I was a teenager, I was a bit awkward...but not anywhere like Tony [Hawk] though, haha.

KVR: Do you have any go-to exercises or physical activities besides skating?

LA: Yeah, I do supplemental training. It's basically all the stuff that skateboarding doesn't work out...I'll aim on hitting those spots. I also do preventative stuff, specifically for my shoulders and ankles to prevent injuries. In the summer and fall, I like to go surfing more often and going on bike rides here and there.

KVR: At what point in your life would you say you were happy with your overall fitness and skills in regards to skating?

LA: When I first started skating and I was just getting into it, I was pretty stoked I was able to lay down a basis for being able to skate, if that makes sense. You just have to practice enough so that eventually you're able to maintain that muscle memory and strength. I think that was the first time I was really happy with my abilities.

At the end of 2013, I tore my CTL in my ankle. After that, I went to therapy for a bunch of treatment. Once I had that injury, I became much more in tune with my body. After I went through all the therapy, I became the most fit I had ever been, so it was crazy to be in that position, especially after that injury. That was also the point when I wanted to pursue skateboarding professionally. I was 21 at that time.

KVR: What keeps you motivated to keep such a high level of fitness?

LA: I just want to feel good on my board. There is a limit though. If you are really strong, that's not necessarily going to help you with your skateboarding. You need to have the skills to go with the strength. As long as I can do what I want to do, that's what matters. The less I'm out of breath and the more my body can keep up with my mind, the better.

Also, it just feels really good to be in good health. I feel like learning how to make use of your body is really important because most people aren't anywhere close to fully using their body. It's pretty sad because you deal with your body your whole life and if you never really understand it and use it, you're not really living.

You gotta keep in mind, you can only (safely) push your body so far and everyone has different ability levels. For example, if I wanted to bike across America, I couldn't just start doing it tomorrow and have my body be okay with that. You gotta train towards it.

KVR: Is there anything you adjust in your training as you prepare for the Olympics?

LA: I've been skating for the past 12 years and I want to implement some exercises to improve my skating, but then I don't want to mix things up too much where stuff gets confusing and I'm creating another problem.

KVR: Did you have anything else you'd like to add regarding health, fitness or eating?

LA: Yeah, sometimes it's hard dealing with changes in diet, especially when I travel. When I got back from Europe, my body reacted differently when I switched foods. You have to listen to your body and a lot of it is mental attitude and good habits. The more you can be mentally strong about something, like eating the right things, the rest will follow.

Landon Donovan

Landon Donovan is a soccer legend. He has had an illustrious professional career playing internationally, in Major League Soccer, and on the US Men's National Team. Landon has a record 6 MLS cups and numerous individual records in both the MLS and on the USMNT. The MLS "Landon Donovan MVP Award" is named in his honor. Currently, he is the Executive Vice President of Soccer Operations for the San Diego Loyal.

FOOD

- Type of eater: Vegetarian, Pescetarian and Omnivore
- Adventurous level: 9

- Taste preferences: salty and spicy
- Ethnicity: mostly European (Irish & English), some African (Nigerian) and some Middle Eastern

KVR: Do you attribute any of your taste preferences to your ethnicity, or is there something else that you give credit to for your tastes?

LD: I would say it's been more environmental/experientially based as opposed to ethnicity...so I think. With the experiences I've had, I've been able to experiment with different things and learned to like different things because of the lifestyle I've lived.

KVR: What are some of your favorite cuisines?

LD: I would say Japanese for sure...sushi for sure. Mexican/Latin food. Those are probably the two I enjoy most.

KVR: Do you follow a certain diet or meal plan, or pretty much eat what you want?

LD: I pretty much eat whatever I want. I try to eat real food, not processed food. Other than that, I kinda just eat what I want. I have pretty good self-control and can gauge when I've been eating too much...Maybe it's time to slow down for a few days or be a little bit healthier for a few days, but I toe that line pretty well.

KVR: Can you give me an example of a typical dish you'll have for each meal of the day?

LD: For breakfast, it's either gluten-free oatmeal with nuts, berries and maybe a banana...or gluten-free cereal with nuts, berries, a banana and almond milk. For lunch, usually a meatless salad (as a general statement). Then for dinner, some sort of vegetable, generally a protein (like salmon or lamb) and some sort of a non-gluten carb (a starch like a potato or sweet potato, rice, quinoa or couscous).

KVR: Do you have any go-to snacks?

LD: I really like these bean chips, "Beanfields" I think they're called. Those would be my go-to. I think it's a mixed bag of beans and they're really good. That or sometimes hard cheese (like gouda), crackers and honey.

KVR: What are some foods that you normally avoid, but crave?

LD: I *love* ice cream, but that kind of dairy does not agree with me. I'm not lactose intolerant, like I'm not going to get sick from it, but I just don't feel good after I eat it. I feel bloated and gross.

My favorite flavors of ice cream are cookies 'n cream, mint chocolate chip and Heath bar.

I love donuts, but I've just got to stay away from it. I love any sort of sweetened breads, cakes, cupcakes...stuff like that.

KVR: What are some of your all-time favorite foods?

LD: I love sushi. I grew up in Southern California, so guacamole is part of who I am as a human being. I love guac. Although I don't eat it a lot, a filet or lamb chop/shank with red wine reduction or a demi-glaze or something like that is just so delicious. I'd say those are my favorites...and a really good burger.

KVR: What are some of your all-time least favorite foods?

LD: They're more obscure...I can't do truffles. I actually don't mind the taste initially, but then I realized that I'd get sick from it so it doesn't smell good to me anymore. Normally I'd like it because I like mushrooms. Weird right?

I'm not a big fan of roe, like salmon roe. I don't like uni (sea urchin). I don't eat any hot dog, SPAM, bologna or any of those processed meats. I pretty much eat everything else.

KVR: What are some of your favorite restaurants?

LD: There are tons. Momofuku Ko, Eleven Madison and Masa in New York. In San Diego, my wife and I love Addison at the Grand Del Mar and Market in Del Mar/Rancho Santa Fe. Trois Mec in LA—

very good. Another really good one in LA is n/naka...They did a Chef's Table episode there. Kitcho Arashiyama in Kyoto, Japan is very very *very* good.

KVR: When you go grocery shopping, do you have any favorite food & beverages you'll usually get?

LD: Definitely guacamole. Lots of vegetables. A lot of beer...love beer. We get most of our beer at the supermarket. Whatever meat or fish we buy, we get from the meat or fish counter.

KVR: How have your eating habits changed over the different phases of your career and retirement?

LD: Dramatically. Well, my eating habits changed commensurate with my learning about food. The more you learn about food and its benefits, the more you realize how bad "not real" food is.

When I was younger, like most people, you're able to eat whatever you want. When you're playing a sport for a living, you feel good and you don't gain weight. But as you get older, you realize how important that is. The more I learned about nutrition and the importance of it, how it would affect my performance, my diet changed dramatically to much cleaner, much healthier foods with a lot more vegetables.

Since I've been retired, it's become a way of life. Now that's the way I eat, for the most part...which is good. With processed foods and drinks, you just learn to not even want them anymore. Once you stop drinking soda for a few years you think, "Why did I ever put this in my body?" Knowledge is power.

FITNESS

KVR: How would you describe your natural body type?

LD: When I was young, before I hit puberty, I was very skinny. Very thin and very lean...mostly because I was so active. Once I hit puberty I got bigger, a little stockier, and that is what my body type is now. Not thick, but a little bit thicker than I was as a kid and definitely athletic from my genes. Spending your life running around a soccer field makes you pretty toned.

Both my parents were athletic. My mom ran track in middle school and high school. My dad was a semi-pro hockey player.

KVR: Do you currently have any go-to exercises or physical activities outside of soccer?

LD: Tennis. That's all I do now. I don't like running. (When there is a ball, there's a lot more involved.) I don't like just straight running. That's boring. I don't like spending time in a gym doing that kinda stuff. I need an engagement of some sort, or a competitive piece to it. So I like playing sports because there's a competitive aspect that's more enjoyable than just sitting and lifting weights and doing things like that. Tennis is what I spend most of my time doing.

KVR: At what point in your life would you say you were happy with your overall fitness?

LD: I would say that happened in two stages. One was probably when I was 22 or 23. I had a really big "a-ha" moment. I read *Fast Food Nation* and from that point on, I never touched soda again, I never touched fast food and that really transformed me. I started feeling much better. As I continued to evolve and learn, I think there was a point in my late 20s where I kinda got it. I figured out that if I eat this, I'm gonna feel great and if I eat that, I'm gonna feel terrible. I was finally in a place where I was knowledgeable to make good decisions. If I did make a bad decision, I would know how it would affect me. Before then, I didn't really put the two together.

KVR: You've been pretty public about battling mental health issues and depression over the years. A common side effect of those affected is the neglect of their physical health by eating poorly and avoiding physical activity. What do you personally do to get back into a healthy mental state?

LD: For me, it's the opposite. If I don't do those things, I'm more inclined to feel depressed. So if I don't work out for a week, I feel myself feeling down and depressed. I can feel it mentally and physically. My wife knows...If it's been 3 or 4 days since my last workout, she'll tell me, "you need to go work out." You produce natural hormones and endorphins when you work out and that helps with mental illness. So, that's what I do if I'm feeling like I'm in a place where I can slip into a more depressed state.

If I'm working out, eating well and not drinking (because alcohol is a depressant), I feel better. I guess you have to have an awareness because you can spiral out of control quickly. It's like when you start to feel down and haven't worked out in a few days, you don't feel good about yourself, so you drink. Then you don't feel good the next day, so you don't want to work out, but then you don't feel good again, so you drink again. You can get into this spiral, so it's important to have the awareness that "Okay, it's been a while. I need to work out, or I shouldn't drink tonight."

KVR: You touched on this, but do you feel that a healthy mental state leads to better fitness or does fitness lead to a better mental state?

LD: Probably both, but for me it's more a better physical state leads to a better mental state. As long as I'm working out and being active (not just working out physically, but my mind is engaged and challenged), I do well. When I'm too sedentary and not active either physically or mentally engaged, then I'm more prone to feeling depressed.

KVR: What has kept you motivated to maintain a high level of fitness?

LD: There was one six-month period of my life after I retired when I could tell I was a little heavier than I've ever been and I just didn't like the feeling. Looking at myself, I didn't like the way I felt. I felt heavier and I didn't like that. You need to have self-awareness because if you're not aware, the next thing you know, you put on 10, 20, or 30 pounds. You see yourself every day, so you don't notice the real changes right away. You have to understand where you really are physically. My motivation is that I don't like feeling that way. It's kinda vain, but it's reality.

KVR: Any other tips regarding health, fitness, eating, or cooking?

LD: I think people get really caught up on diets or a certain way of eating and I never really understood that. If you need a certain way of eating or a certain way of doing something to motivate yourself, it's not going to be sustainable. So, I think that looking at the whole picture and understanding the mental, physical and emotional aspects all together allows you to choose your options in a healthy way all around. It doesn't mean you're eating vegetables and fish all day. It means, "Ok, I've been eating well for the last week and I really want a donut, so I'm gonna eat a donut...because mentally, it's going to make me feel really good tonight." So, I think understanding the whole picture is important as opposed to being stuck into one certain way of eating.

Knowing yourself and knowing what works is especially important. I love *love* bread and pasta, but I know when I eat things like that, I feel more bloated and inflamed. Sometimes I do it...The other night at dinner, I ate a bunch of bread because I worked out, I was really hungry and I wanted to eat it. I know I'm gonna feel inflamed afterwards, but it's okay. It was worth it.

It's about understanding your body well. I know I don't do well with dairy, so if I eat cheese I know I'm not gonna feel good. I make that decision when I need to. Understanding your body really well is important, knowing what works and doesn't work. If you're not aware of any of it and you're going for three straight days going "Huh, I don't feel well. I wonder what's happening. Maybe I'm sick." Well, maybe it's because you ate this, that and the other and if you're not aware of it, you're never going to know how to fix it.

For a good recipe, it's nothing groundbreaking, but I love making either a beef shank or lamb shank slow-roasted or braised. I make it with a bunch of veggies and sear the shank and add either a veggie broth or chicken broth, red wine and tomato paste. Then I put it in the oven or on the stove for 3-5 hours and let it slow roast. It peels off the bone. I love that with sweet potato mash. It's really good because it gives a good sweetness to the saltiness. I love broccolini—it goes great with that. Doesn't that sound good?

Festus Ezeli

Festus Ezeli is a professional athlete and NBA (National Basketball Association) Champion. He won the 2015 NBA Finals with the Golden State Warriors and had previously played NCAA Division 1 basketball for the Vanderbilt Commodores.

FOOD

- Type of eater: Omnivore, Pescetarian, Vegan—honestly, it changes depending on the time of the year and what I'm training for
- Adventurous level: 7—I've watched a lot of cooking and travel shows and I definitely don't want to eat anything that's alive, so if that's a 10, then I'm a 7. I'm staying away from that.
- Taste preference: sweet, salty, spicy, bitter, sour and savory— I like EVERYTHING. (Although when I first came to the US,

I hated BBQ sauce because I didn't understand the mixture of sweet and savory. Then I went to school down South in Nashville. I got used to it and now it tastes amazing to me.)

- Ethnicity: Nigerian—I was born in Nigeria in West Africa.

KVR: Do you attribute any of your taste preferences to your ethnicity? Is there something else that you give credit to for your tastes?

FE: Yes, I usually go for things that have a lot of flavor and that comes from our cultural foods and the way I grew up. I know that the love for spices (really hot spices) comes from that.

I give credit to my mom for sure. My dad loves my mom's cooking, so his appetite and his taste for really hot food with a lot of peppers really made an impact on me. The credit goes to both my parents!

And living in the Bay Area accustomed me to even more diversity. Food is a way of life and when we sit to break bread, we get to bond with loved ones and that is really important to me.

KVR: What are your favorite cuisines?

FE: Obviously, I really love Nigerian food. That's my #1 favorite cuisine. We have a lot of rice dishes. We have fried rice and jollof rice, which is really similar to Spanish rice, but more flavorful. We also have fufu, which is a ball of flour that you eat with different kinds of soups. Fufu comes in different forms...They could be yams, plantains, or oatmeal mashed together and eaten with your hands. It's a delicacy in Africa as a whole and every country has its own version that's native to them.

A close second is Asian Fusion. That's one of my big favorites. There was a place next door to my place in Oakland and I was there every day. It was a Korean-Mexican fusion place called "Belly" and it was really, really good.

Other than that, I love everything! I love Thai food. I love Greek...That's actually new for me. Hummus is amazing. Also, southern barbecue is always a plus. There's really nothing I can't eat. I love food!

KVR: Do you follow a certain diet, meal plan, make sure to avoid/include certain foods, or pretty much eat whatever you want?

FE: Because of my track of recovering from an injury, I have to really be careful with the foods I eat. With training, rehab and trying to stay in shape; I have to follow a certain way of eating. I eat way more protein like fish and way more veggies than I normally consume. I also eat a little bit of carbs, but the carbs usually come from the ground (e.g. potatoes, plantains and rice).

KVR: Can you give me an example of a typical dish you'll have for breakfast, lunch and dinner? Any go-to snacks?

FE: My breakfast is consistent. It's always the same, oatmeal and eggs...every day. If I want to switch it up, I'll throw some nuts in there or a banana. Sometimes I'll add almond milk. Lunch is usually tuna and a mix of veggies (e.g. garbanzo beans, kale, spinach and beets). For dinner, I love having plantains, potatoes, or sweet potatoes. I'll mix and match those with veggies and either chicken or fish. That's how my diet usually goes every day. There's a little tweaking here and there with different kinds of proteins and veggies, but it stays pretty consistent.

For snacks, there's different kinds of nuts I'll eat. Actually, when I first got drafted to the NBA, I met with a nutritionist for the first time. My diet wasn't the best in college. I could eat whatever I wanted. I felt that I worked so hard and worked out so much that it never showed on my body. In fact, I needed to eat more to gain weight so I would eat all this crazy stuff. It wasn't until I met with a nutritionist that I was educated on what I was putting in my body. The thing was, I loved cookies. I used to eat cookies by the dozens and obviously that isn't normal. Now that I think about it, I used to buy them by the cartons. My nutritionist had to help me get rid of that obsession with cookies and breads by replacing them with nuts and other healthier snacks in between meals. That was the biggest change for me as a pro athlete.

KVR: What are some foods you normally avoid, but crave...like cheat day foods?

FE: I love Southern comfort foods: fried chicken, mashed potatoes, mac and cheese, collard greens and sweet potatoes (they always come in one way or another). I love fries...Those are my favorite. Boba tea. Ice cream. Those are all foods that I'll usually avoid day-to-day, but on a cheat day in the summer after the season's over, you can relax a little bit and have some of those things and reward yourself. I'll have those things very sparingly because I know how much of a sweet tooth I have and how addicted I can be to them. It can get pretty out of hand.

KVR: What are some of your all-time favorite foods?

FE: I'm so lucky because my mom makes so much great food that I don't feel like I'm missing anything from my daily diet. My favorite Nigerian food is pounded yam and egusi soup. I could eat that every day for the next year and be totally fine. The pounded yam is essentially a harder form of mashed potatoes. It's harder because you have to be able to grab it with your hands. Then you dip it in the egusi soup which is made from melon seeds and has a lot of flavor with the veggies, meat (i.e. chicken, beef, goat or snail) and whatever else they put in there in the Nigerian way.

KVR: What are some of your all-time least favorite foods?

FE: I don't like any dessert with apples, peaches or anything that could get soggy. Something about that consistency is not my thing! However, my all-time favorite desserts are anything with bananas. Anything with bananas and coconut...then you've got me. Banana bread? Forget about it. That's how my friends entice me to do things I don't want to do. They'll bake me banana bread. It's so good to me...and if you add some coconut to make it even better, I'm putty. I'm just goo in their hands.

KVR: What are some of your favorite restaurants and why?

FE: Like I said earlier, one of them was next to my place in Oakland...Belly. I was there after practice EVERY DAY. They have these amazing burritos and tacos. It was Asian Fusion so, for example, they have a Cali burrito which has fries, chicken, rice and all these different ingredients that I didn't think went on burritos but tasted great together; that place is amazing. I also love Brown Sugar Kitchen in Oakland because I love breakfast in general.

I love Ike's Sandwiches. It was a place I got addicted to when I was in the Bay. I went there so much, Ike became a good friend of mine. If you go there, you should get "The Festus."

In San Francisco, I love eating at State Bird Provisions with our guy, Joco. That place is amazing.

I love the sushi at Mikuni in Sacramento. Oh! And there's also a new place in Sacramento called Bawk!, which is a really good fried chicken spot.

In Nashville, there's a really good southern food place called Monell's. It is incredible. That's a place I would take my family whenever they were in town. If I keep naming restaurants, we'll be here all day.

KVR: When you go grocery shopping, do you have any favorite food & beverage products that you'll often get?

FE: I only go grocery shopping for fruits and veggies. That's my job because I'm the one very picky eater in the house when it comes to that. Other people take care of the rest of the food, but I'll make sure to get oranges, bananas, avocados (I love avocados!), pears, grapes, kale and spinach (for smoothies) and kombucha.

Oh, and I love hummus. I have to go to Trader Joe's for that though. It's so good! I fell in love with hummus when my brothers and I went to Barcelona a year ago. I got some hummus as a snack. It was so good that I bought every container of that type of hummus. We were only in Barcelona for five days. We ate that whole thing in three days. One of these days I will try to make hummus homemade.

KVR: You touched on this earlier talking about how you didn't eat the healthiest food in college, but how have your eating habits changed over your career from college to the pros?

FE: As a young college guy, based on your workload, you feel like you can eat whatever you want and do whatever you want and get away with it, which you can temporarily. I ate anything and everything. My plate used to be a mash of all kinds of food. My teammates used to make fun of me about how much I could eat. At the end of the day, I didn't really think about it because I was trying to put weight on and sustain my energy. I also noticed, at that time, my sleep was weird because I would eat late at night and I just didn't know any better. I would always work out at night and I would always be the last one to leave the gym, so I always would get home late. My best friend at the time would work out with me and we'd get home around midnight and our tradition was to eat cereal and just talk it up...talk about the day. You would never see me eat cereal now because it can be harmful to your body. It's kind of like cardboard with sugar on it. These are things I've come to understand.

When I got to the pros, they start educating us on what was good for our bodies. In college, we played 30 games. In the pros, we now played 82 games. So, we had to be more regimented with our diets. With our travel schedule, we'd also get into cities past midnight and I also got to learn that there are things you can and cannot eat past midnight if we wanted to have a productive next day. These were things that I never used to think about.

The role that vegetables play in your diet is very important for everybody. But for athletes, we put this demand on our bodies at such a high rate that we HAVE to eat more veggies. We have to eat more fruits. We have to put things in our bodies that build our bodies up. A lot of people just eat without thinking that the body needs to rebuild. That's why so many people end up with different crazy diseases because they just eat to satisfy hunger. That's something I would really love to change; I'd really like to change that mentality.

Just the idea of how much we're putting into our healthcare...We spend so much money at the hospital when we could be spending that money on eating healthier foods and living a healthier lifestyle. Those are things I always preach to kids about. People will say "Oh they're just kids. They can get away with eating all these cookies and snacks." The thing is, whatever you put in your body early in life can build bad habits that you'll pay the consequences for later in life. Now, you don't have to cut out the treats completely, but at least add more veggies and foods that are nutritious for your body. That would be a great conversation for people to hear and be a part of.

Whatever gets instilled in you, you carry through your life. When I was younger, I knew cookies were bad for your teeth, but I didn't know they were actually bad for your body, your joints and all these different ailments and diseases you can suffer from later in life like arthritis and diabetes. All these body pains can come from all the sugars that we eat. I've tried my best to educate myself by talking to nutritionists and watching videos and documentaries on these things.

I don't want to sit here and talk about all these "bad things." I still want to enjoy everything, but in moderation. So, for every ice cream I eat, I'll have two plates of something green to compensate. That's how I think now in that regard and it's been working pretty well.

FITNESS

KVR: How would you describe your natural body type? Lean, athletic, or stocky?

FE: Lean and athletic.

KVR: Do you have any go-to exercises or physical activities?

FE: My job is basketball, so that's my go-to. But other than that, I do a lot of boxing, riding bikes and whatever will break up that monotonous nature that basketball puts on your body and will keep my body in shape.

KVR: How have your exercises evolved over the years?

FE: It's all about education, so the older I get and the more I learn, the more I understand the need to take care of my body. As a young guy in high school or college, you just think: the more you do, the better you are. So, you lift all the weights you can, you play all the basketball you can and you run as much as you can. Yes, these things are great, but you also have to do as much of the necessary recovery as you can.

When I became a pro, I started doing more yoga since I started having more injuries. I also do Pilates. I do boxing which is great for the core...and now I'm learning the importance of that. These are things that I have put into my routine. Icing your joints and your knees while getting the appropriate rest is important. Sleep is especially important; it's so, *so* important. You have to make sure you're taking care of your body as much as you're demanding from it.

KVR: At what point in your life were you happy with your overall fitness?

FE: Yeah, since becoming a pro, every year in basketball by mid-season is when I feel like I've been getting into my peak, especially going into the playoffs. I'm at a good place when I've been training, playing at a high level and have kept my diet locked in.

I think that as the season starts to go on, with our sleep patterns all over the place and fatigue setting in, maybe then performance starts to drop off. But I think that somewhere just before the middle of the season, you start to hit that peak...and that's for pretty much everybody. The game is more of a battle of attrition than just skill or will. You have to be able to take care of your body. In the NBA these days, with the level of talent and competition on every team, the healthiest man wins.

KVR: You've gone through your fair share of ups and downs in your career, from winning an NBA championship to rebuilding yourself from a debilitating knee injury. What keeps you motivated to maintain such a high level of fitness?

FE: First of all, I'm a competitor so I want to be the best. That, in itself, is enough for you to work your hardest, make sure you're in tip-top shape and make sure you work on your diet and your sleep. You want to win games and you want to be an asset to your team. That's my main reason.

Secondly, I feel like a role model to kids. They watch me and see if I'm living healthily. I have a Thanksgiving meal every year and the kids watch me and see what I put on my plate. Whenever I post what I'm eating on Instagram, people watch that. So, it's also about practicing what you preach.

But again, my motivation for being at my peak performance is mostly because of my competitive nature and I also want to live a healthy life. Those are both things that really drive me and has a lot to do with mental health. Taking care of my mental health is a priority to me.

KVR: Do you have anything you want to add...any tips or advice regarding health & fitness, eating, or cooking?

FE: Honestly, when it comes to food, I've been moving away from eating out because I want to be so sure of what I'm putting into my body. Nobody has all the answers and everybody's different, but one thing I do know is that the healthier I eat (or what I consider to be healthy—whether it's eating more veggies and fruits or sometimes tinkering with my diet), the better I feel. So, I do things to make my body feel good. I challenge everyone to educate themselves and do whatever it is that makes their bodies feel good, not just eating what tastes good.

We have to keep feeding ourselves with the right foods and making sure that our bodies are healthy. That's the only way we can perform. We ask so much of our bodies. We push them every day with work...working 9-to-5 and not getting enough sleep, then coming back the next day demanding the same output. It's the same thing with workouts. I have friends who run all these crazy marathons, then come out of it and eat junk. I'm thinking to myself, "You're breaking your body down." You have to eat foods that will build that body back up. It's not until later when they're struggling with injuries that they look for solutions...and I've dealt with my fair share of injuries, so I know. I understand how I used to eat and the effects that has had on my body. For me, it's about educating people so they don't have to go through the same process that I went through. Our job is such that as we learn, we teach someone and as they learn more, they'll teach someone else. That's how we'll all become better.

Tony Hawk

Tony Hawk is a skateboarding legend. As a pioneer of vert skateboarding, he was the first to successfully land the 900 (2 ½ aerial revolutions on a skateboard ramp). He's also widely known for his best-selling "Tony Hawk's" video game series. He is the CEO of Birdhouse and the founder of the Tony Hawk Foundation.

FOOD

- Type of eater: Omnivore
- Adventurous level: 9 or 10—I've had a tarantula, but I hesitate to say "10" just cause someone would probably test me on that

and say "Will you eat this live frog?" Then I'll be like, "Uh, maybe not that."

- Taste preference: spicy
- Ethnicity: Caucasian, mostly European. I did the whole 23andMe, but I honestly don't remember all the details. There's a little Native American somewhere in there too, but I wouldn't claim that in a way a politician does. It's very minimal.

KVR: Do you attribute any of your taste preferences to your ethnicity, or is there something else that you give credit to for your tastes?

TH: My travels. Growing up, my mom and dad weren't too adventurous. We ate a lot of fast food. Going out to a meal was like going to Bob's Big Boy—that was kinda like livin' it up. It wasn't some great culinary option or desire. It was just very American. So, when I traveled back when I was a teenager and younger, everything seemed strange and weird so I didn't really embrace it. But as I grew older, I came to really appreciate the diversity of the different tastes and cuisines from all over the world. At some point, I just fell in love with it all. Now that's sort of my motivating factor for traveling. Skating is just incidental to being able to eat at some really nice places.

KVR: What are some of your favorite cuisines?

TH: Ooh, that's tricky. I really like a lot of Asian cuisines: Japanese, Thai and Indian. But I also love Ethiopian food and "fusion" stuff that people come up with now that has no particular geographic origin.

KVR: Do you follow a certain diet, meal plan, or do you pretty much eat whatever you want?

TH: I don't have a specific diet. I guess my only diet is moderation. I like to try everything, but not indulge myself too much and try to keep it on the healthy side. I try to stay active. I saw my dad's health diminish so much and I blame a lot of it on his diet through the years. That was an example for me that you can't always eat prime rib, burgers and greasy...everything. So, I watched him and was like alright, I gotta try to be cognizant of "how much" and "how often."

I don't follow any sort of regimen, wellness program, or anything like that. It's pretty much just watch your intake and stay active. That's pretty much it.

KVR: Can you give me an example of typical dishes you'll have throughout the day for breakfast, lunch and dinner?

TH: For breakfast, usually when I'm traveling, I'll have whatever version of oatmeal they have and a croissant...unless there's a specialty that you have to try on the menu. For lunch, I'll have a gyro pita sandwich with "hummus in" as a special request. That's typical for me at work. Other times, I'll go to this really good fish taco place nearby. There's also a place called Plant Power, it's a vegan place. I explore everything, but I think it's one of the best places.

KVR: Any go-to snacks?

I don't snack much. The extent of it would be these Milton crackers that my kids like and hummus. I also eat those pre-packaged salami, cheese and cracker things that are everywhere now. I used to make that and get all the ingredients separately, but once I saw that packaged I was like, "Alright, that's speaking to me."

KVR: Are there any foods that you normally avoid, but crave...like "cheat day" foods?

TH: I'm not above driving to McDonald's and getting a #2. Other than that, Roberto's burritos are kind of a guilty pleasure.

KVR: What are some of your all-time favorite foods?

TH: Gosh that's hard. I love tasting menus. I love good Indian food. There's a sushi place in LA called Sushi Zo and it's omakase so they serve sushi (usually nigiri) one at a time. It's always one of the best experiences I've had.

KVR: What are your all-time least favorite foods?

TH: I'm not a fan of significant amounts of cilantro or chopped onions, especially if they're not grilled. I feel chopped onions just overpower the taste of almost any dish, especially if they're fresh. I avoid them if I can, but I know sometimes I can't.

I've had it and I've tried it, but I'm not a big fan of sweetbreads...the thyroid glands and stuff like that.

KVR: What are some of your favorite restaurants and why?

TH: In San Diego, for sure it's Market Del Mar and Herb & Wood downtown.

I love Beauty and Essex in New York. In fact, they just opened one in Vegas. Also, I love Blue Ribbon Brasserie in New York.

Probably one of my all-time favorite go-to's is Matsuhisa in LA. It's Nobu's first restaurant and still the most creative...and he's there. He pops in sometimes. Matsuhisa's omakase is next level.

I love good barbecue too, but it's rare to find in our area.

KVR: When you go grocery shopping, do you have any favorite foods and beverages that you'll often get?

TH: I just try to get the basics in terms of the things my kids are gonna eat. My first stop at the grocery store is usually cereal. We usually get honey corn flakes. I don't know what the brand is, but it's honey corn flakes.

We also get a lot of chips and a lot of fruits. Also, I'll usually get a 12-pack of Cokes that I kinda hide from my kids since I'll have them every once in a while, but they usually pilfer them.

KVR: At 50 years young...when you reflect back on your eating habits, what would you tell that adolescent skater with the knowledge and experience you have now?

TH: I would say, try to embrace the opportunities you have as soon as possible. I feel like I didn't really learn to appreciate or embrace the opportunities I had until much later in life. I probably would have enjoyed the travel a lot more at a younger age. It always felt like a big burden to be traveling for 4-5 weeks at a time through Europe or Australia. Knowing what I know now and not having the obligations of being a parent, it would have made those trips a lot more enjoyable.

Now, because I'm a parent and I have obligations, I don't want to go away for 4-5 weeks at a time. I'm just not gonna enjoy it like that.

FITNESS

KVR: How would you describe your natural body type? Lean, athletic, stocky?

TH: I would say "lean."

KVR: **As a vert skater, do you have any go-to exercises or physical activities, or do you pretty much just skateboard?**

TH: Nah, just skating. I kinda have a warm-up routine that I do that gives me a sense of what I'm capable of, or what I need to work on that day. If I'm already "in tune," I'll jump into harder stuff. So I have a test run to let me know how my body's doing.

KVR: **I know your son, Riley, is into this, but do you ever venture into street skating?**

TH: Sometimes with my other kids, but over the last 10-15 years I get hurt way more often street skating and roll my ankles a lot. I've come to realize that if I really want to continue skating, I've got to stick with what I'm good at and don't usually get hurt on...which is ramps.

KVR: **At what point were you happy with your overall fitness and skills?**

TH: I think in my mid-30s, when we were doing our Boom Boom Huckjam tours, I was at my peak...not just in fitness, but in skating. All the tricks felt relatively easy. I could do them on command and in front of crowds. I wasn't concerned so much about the injuries and as

I endured a couple of major injuries after that, those tricks became a lot harder to summon or perform.

KVR: How long did it take for you to get to that point of reaching your peak? How many years of training?

TH: It was a combination of skating consistently through the years and ending my competition. Ending competition, in general, freed me to try harder things and skate in a different way that wasn't so conservative. I think that was the catalyst for me being able to do these incredibly difficult things more frequently in a show format.

I competed almost 20 years up to that point in my life. I was skating well in competition, but freeing myself of that opened up so much opportunity in how to skate. Once I was free of that and doing this creative show called The Huckjam, it allowed me to really explore a whole new style and push my limits much further than I already knew.

KVR: What exactly keeps you motivated to maintain such a high level of fitness and skill?

TH: The baseline is that I enjoy it. Skating has always been my #1 activity and the thing I've felt the most confident in. Now, it's just skating on a regular basis to keep in shape and keep my skill set fresh. I don't think of it as a job. I truly enjoy it.

Once in a while, I'm asked to do stuff that isn't my most comfortable way of skating or what I'm good at...So in those instances, it becomes more like a job. For example, they'll want me to do an exhibition at a skate park and everything in the park is relatively small, including the pool that everyone loves to skate. Because it's so small, it's very limiting for my trick options. It's like I have to struggle to do basic things. On any given day, for fun, I wouldn't be doing that.

KVR: What common misconceptions do you think people have that might potentially limit them when it comes to food or fitness?

TH: Mostly that they are not capable of doing something that they probably are capable of if they are willing to put in the time and effort to learn or do it. Everything takes discipline, including eating. If they can find that strength in them to be disciplined about their eating, that's hugely important. I feel like, through my years, I was so disciplined in my skating that I never understood how that could translate into anything else in my life...in terms of personal life, eating, or chemical use. At some point, I made that shift when I realized, "Oh, I have this discipline. I just have to learn to use it in other ways."

I think other people just have to find that within themselves, where are they disciplined in their life and how they can translate that into being healthy.

KVR: Is there anything else you want to add...maybe a recipe you want to share?

TH: I don't cook. I just enjoy everyone else who is an expert at it, especially since I don't want to take the time to actually prepare it. That's kind of what I've resigned to...I'm good at eating.

Apolo Ohno

Apolo Ohno is a legendary speed skater and is the most decorated American Winter Olympian of all time (as an 8x Olympic medalist). He has been an ambassador for the Special Olympics, a motivational speaker and philanthropist.

FOOD

- Type of eater: Omnivore, Carnivore, Pollotarian, Pescetarian—I identify with all of these depending on the time of the year and what type of eating pattern I'm currently following. I would say the least amount of my time spent in any of these eating regimes is vegetarian or vegan. I tend to eat meat frequently, but less and less red meat as I get older.

- Adventurous level: 11—I've eaten some pretty weird stuff in Asia...anything that has to do with the throat or the tongue of an animal.

- Taste preferences: Sour and savory. I try to avoid sweets. Depending on what sweetener you use, it can be highly addictive.

- Ethnicity: My father is Japanese. My grandfather and grandmother are both Japanese, so my lineage is quite strong and deep on that side. The other half is a mix and blend of European: British, Irish, speckles of Italian and some Scandinavian as well.

KVR: Do you attribute any of your taste preferences to your ethnicity, or is there something else that you give credit to for your tastes?

AO: I think the tastes that I have, for sure in the Asian genres of food, are there because my father introduced me at a very young age to a wide plethora of different cuisines. However, I think my curiosity stems from my pure travels and my openness to accept these different cultures, foods and histories of eating these types of foods...as well as the stories behind them. Plus, I've had a deep profound curiosity about culture, people, what they ate and for what reasons. Furthermore, this highlights my fascination with global travel and the foods we eat around the world and the reasons for the stories behind them.

KVR: What are some of your favorite cuisines?

AO: Anything in Asia, whether that's local Singaporean, Malay, Chinese...I love Japanese food, love Korean food and love Hong Kong food. I love Vietnamese food and Thai food. But then, I have a profound deep respect for Italian food and for food that is typically south of the border like Mexican food. I'm a foodie, so I love to eat food and the more authentic and hand-made that food is, the more my belly gets full.

KVR: Do you follow a certain diet or meal plan, or eat pretty much what you want?

AO: I'm quite realistic in terms of my approach towards food. Obviously, when I was competing, I was extremely regimented and strict. However, during the past ten years of my career I've loved to indulge.

I believe life should be lived fruitfully and fully so I'll never push away a meal because I'm following a strict diet. Hence, when I do travel,

I'm not on the quasi-health wagon, so I'm not eating as strict. When I travel, I try to take in as much as I can.

Although there are a few trips, if I'm feeling like I need to cut it back and tone it down, I will eat very specific to what my normal plan is just in terms of the food groups. I try to stay away from anything that's artificial or has a lot of sugar or is just loaded with carbohydrates. I try to stay away from those things because I tend to not feel good after eating them, as much as I love them...But it's not like I'm going to go to Italy and not eat bowls of pasta and pizza, or go to France and not eat bread. It's just not gonna happen. I will fully *fully* appreciate and live in those moments. Then, when I come back home to Los Angeles or Hong Kong or wherever I'm based at that time, I will dial it back to a stricter regime again. That way I feel comfortable and operate well. I've experienced that it's more fun when I go to all these different places around the world and can appreciate the food so much more because I haven't been eating like that for a long time. So I *can* indulge. I *can* experience it. I *can* really enjoy myself...versus if I ate like that all the time, it probably wouldn't taste as good because I'm just so used to it. Moderation, right? I spike my system. I shock it.

KVR: What is an example of a typical dish you'll have for each meal of the day?

AO: Well, I don't typically have breakfast. I'll usually have water, sparkling water, coffee (black) or tea (plain with nothing added) in the morning. I'll usually have my first meal anywhere from noon to 3 p.m. and that's usually some sort of small salad with some type of a protein and maybe some berries, other fruits and nuts. That's pretty typical. Then for dinner, depending on if I'm eating at home or if I'm eating out, I'll try to stick to some kind of a meat or protein...and again, more vegetables and a salad. That's pretty much it. It's pretty simple.

KVR: Do you have any go-to snacks?

AO: I love to snack, but I've been trying to wean myself off of continuously stuffing my face with calories throughout the day. I try to just use the time-restricted feeding model and stick with the hours that I'm actually supposed to be eating. I try to stay lower on the carbohydrate scale...although sometimes it's difficult because my girlfriend is half Italian and she makes an amazing carbonara. But for the most part, I feel that I operate at my best when I'm eating lower amounts of carbohydrates and my blood sugar and insulin levels are very stable from eating a plethora of green alkaline-based foods and clean protein sources.

KVR: What are some foods that you would normally avoid, but crave? Do you have any "cheat day" foods?

AO: Yeah, I think anything that's in the donut category or the sandwich category counts (cause you're eating a lot of processed meat and bread). Anything that's heavy in carbohydrates and fat tends not to be on my list of foods I normally eat. But then again, I love foods that are very oily too, like Chinese hot pot. It's usually cooked in a very spicy sauce and then dipped again in another oil dip. I love that food.

However, I do think I have something called a "hypoabsorption ability." So when I eat a lot of lipids, my blood lipid profile can spike very easily if I'm eating a lot of very high fatty foods, or eating a lot of oil. So, I have to be very cognizant of that.

It's like everyone else...I try to stay away from donuts, stay away from ice cream and stay away from anything in the white bread or starches category as much as I possibly can. When I'm training really hard, or I'm hitting a really difficult workout of the day and have been doing it for many days in a row, I do tend to crave higher carbohydrate meals, just because I'm so depleted in glycogen.

But usually when I'm on that healthy wagon, it's pretty easy to maintain. I think we've found that when you are fueling your body with the right types of nutrients, you actually eliminate a lot of these cravings. These cravings come because you've been fueling yourself with those sugars or those carbohydrates for so long, so your fuel partitioning has been so used to using them as a fuel source versus using these high-quality nutrients.

It's all about switching that fuel source and making sure your body is used to it and recognizes that it does not need to be fully stuffed all the time with these bad nutrients versus getting really high-quality, densely packed nutrients that taste great, make you feel good and allow you to operate at a very high level.

Food is a drug, right? Your body responds to social media, to working out, to friends and relationships...just like it would with food. When you eat something that reminds you of being a kid, whether it's ice cream or a candy bar or a donut or pizza...during those first probably 2-3 minutes of consuming that, it's an amazing feeling. Unfortunately, then you get that full feeling and usually there's that sense of remorse. The double whammy is that you've told your body, "Hey, there's lots and lots of carbohydrate storage here. We don't know the next time you're going to eat. Therefore, let's start storing all these carbohydrates and sugars in our system because we're not sure when we're gonna get this type of shock overload again." Hence, it's very difficult to burn that off. So, just because you smash a large pizza (which I've done many times by the way), it's not like you can just go for a run the next day to burn that off. It doesn't work, unfortunately. It takes a much longer system.

There's no substitute for consistency. That's why, whether it's me or someone else who's trying to achieve some lifestyle goals, it is exactly what's stated...This is a lifestyle. This is consistent. You can't make up eating badly for a full week by having two really hard workouts. The body does not work that way. Every year that you age, your body has a lesser and lesser ability to dispose of that excess glucose in the system and you just have to be more careful. I'm guilty of it, like many other people, but the older I get, the more I recognize the importance of maintaining some consistency and also just having some balance...knowing that I have the mental capability of being able to reign in that so-called "monkey mind" that wants to dance all over the place and eat whatever it wants because I'm not a young 17-year-old anymore who has this incredible metabolism to burn through anything as if it was cardboard and use it as fuel. So that's what I think is the most important thing.

Americans have been kind of misled for generations about the way we're supposed to eat, what these different pyramid groups are supposed to look like and what is the most effective way for each of us individually to eat that is going to be sustainable for us to eat in the long term. There will always be crash diets, fads and trends...That's fine, but I think it's important to eat balanced throughout life with foods full of great macronutrients. I'm not opposed to supplements. I think supplements are fantastic, but I think the first and foremost change that needs to happen is the actual food that you're eating on a daily basis and your decision-making process...and that always starts with your mind. If your mind is not clear and you are operating in a state of deficiency (and that can be a wide array of things), the decision-making process becomes difficult. We gotta get people off of these addictive sugar diets and get them back into a state of homeostasis through great hydration, through great sleep and all the things that we know, including exercise and consistency.

There's nothing wrong with enjoying chocolate or ice cream or these things. It's just the abundance at which people are consuming them and the consistency at which people are consuming them...That usually tends to be the problem. So, if you're someone like me, who has a difficulty with moderation, you've got to have a very strong mental capability of turning that light switch on or off. So you should be able to say, "Look, I'm on the wagon. Nothing is going to detract me from eating this specific way during this specific time." Then when you're off, you're enjoying it and you're not beating yourself up over eating whatever that not-so-healthy meal was. It's also really important for people to recognize having that cognitive understanding that, "I know what this is doing to my body and I know that this can only be done in light moderation." I don't think that we know that because we haven't been properly taught what it is to eat clean, what it is to eat well and why it's so important for us in the long term. Many times, we've been given the wrong information.

KVR: What are some of your all-time favorite foods?

AO: I think it's all those things I've kind of listed, haha. I'm a Gemini by nature, so every week is different. I may have a new flavor of the week in terms of what I'm craving. For a while it was Middle Eastern food, then it was Chinese food, then it was Italian food, then it was Japanese food, then it was Vietnamese food, then it was Thai. I've been blessed and lucky enough to experience all those cultures in person to experience and taste that authenticity. I guess it just depends on my mood. I like everything though. There's not one food culture that I just don't like or that I'm not happy with.

KVR: Do you have any all-time least favorite foods?

AO: Number one is pretzels. If I was starving on an island, I'd rather starve than eat any kind of pretzel. Anything pretzel-based is out...No shot. I don't know why. Two, I do not like black olives. I am also not a fan of cauliflower. I've had it many, many different ways. I don't know what it is...just not a fan. I do not like sweet pickles either. I like sour pickles, just not sweet pickles.

KVR: What are some of your favorite restaurants and why?

AO: That's a great question. There are many. One of the restaurants is my girlfriend's restaurant in Andersonville, just north of Chicago called Bar Roma. It's a combination of really really good Italian food and atmosphere. So it's not stuffy. It's very much family-style...very communal. The food is excellent. The quality of the food is very high and that makes me happy. I'm a real stickler when it comes to the quality of the ingredients of the food, so I tend to want to know, "Where the meat is coming from? Where are the vegetables coming from? Are they are organic or not? If they're not organic, where are they sourced from?" That's important to me.

KVR: When you're out grocery shopping, do you have any favorite foods or beverages that you'll usually get?

AO: It's always the same. It's usually lemons, lettuce, cabbage, olive oil, apple cider vinegar, feta cheese, parmesan, eggs, chicken, red meat of some sort (if I do get it), That's about it. Sometimes sardines. Sometimes nuts. It's very plain...but I'm a good cook! I just don't cook that extravagant, unless my girlfriend's craving it. She'll say, "I want something besides your salad every day." But honestly, that's how to stick to a healthy diet. That's how to maintain consistency...You stop buying all the other stuff that you just don't need. Simplicity is king in sticking to something. You need to make it very easy to make it consistent.

KVR: How have your eating habits changed since retiring from competitive speed skating, if at all?

AO: They've changed immensely. I'm much more open because I'm doing so much more business internationally, so I'm always being hosted over a meal in some capacity. I'm also much more adventurous.

When I was training as an athlete, I would eat the same things every single day within five minutes of each other. I had to carry my own food with me. It was always the same thing and the same amount. It was very very very strict. That was what was required because I wasn't eating food for taste, unfortunately. It was purely for fuel. So whatever the highest octane quality of fuel was going to go in my body, that's what I was consuming.

I've always loved food, but during that period in my life, that's what it took (in my eyes) to really separate me from others. I had to go to that extreme and try to shave inches off of my recovery time.

FITNESS

KVR: How would you describe your natural body type?

AO: I'm naturally athletic, but I'm not super tall so I'm not naturally lean. I am shorter and most of the exercises I do are either running, biking or lifting...some sort of a circuit. So I tend to build muscle very easily.

KVR: About how much time did you spend working out when you were speed skating versus now?

AO: Back in the day, that's all I did. Actual physical training, we did 2-3 hours in the morning, rest, 2-3 hours in the afternoon and 1 hour in the evening. So probably 6-7 hours a day. Now, I'd say 45 minutes to an hour at the most. Six days a week.

KVR: You already touched on this briefly, but what are some of your go-to exercises or physical activities?

AO: I will run. I will bike. I will do intervals. I will do anything that requires a push, a pull, a lift and a set down. Very basic movements. That can be a kettlebell swing, a kettlebell snatch, a deadlift, a squat, a hip hinge, a push press, a pushup, a hang clean...Those are pretty much all the exercises, nothing else.

KVR: At what point in your life would you say you were actually happy with your overall fitness? How long did it take for you to get to that point?

AO: For sure in my Olympic years. I was outrageously fit. It took my whole life up until that point…The first half of my life, for sure.

KVR: It has been years since you've been a competitive speed skater. What has kept you motivated to maintain your fitness today?

AO: I wouldn't consider I have a high level of fitness (as compared to when I was competing), but I just think "life." I want to be 70, 80, 90 years old and I want to be strong & fit and healthy & happy. Those are very important things to me. No longer is it important to go fast in circles on ice, or to look a certain way…It's more functional fitness and longevity for me.

KVR: Do you have anything else you'd like to add? Any tips on health, fitness, eating or cooking?

AO: I think first and foremost is to keep it simple. I think people overcomplicate what they should and shouldn't do. Generally speaking, I think everyone knows the foods that they should stay away from and everyone understands the foods that they probably should eat more of. That includes a lot of dark green vegetables. Stay away from sugars. Stay away from heavy amounts of carbohydrates. Once you eliminate most of those things from your diet, the results are dramatic. From there, you can start to dive a little bit deeper.

Keeping it simple is the best way to keep something consistent and sustainable. Remember, at the end of the day, the most powerful tool that you have in your arsenal is your mind. You may not recognize this now, but your mind is extremely powerful and it's capable of things that far exceed your own personal expectations of your potential.

Michael Olajide, Jr.

Michael Olajide, Jr. a.k.a. "Silk" is a former middleweight champion boxer and international fitness expert. He is the Co-Founder of AEROSPACE in New York City and the father of AEROMETHODOLOGY. He has trained all his clients (from NYC locals to Victoria's Secret supermodels and A-list actors) like professional athletes to achieve their ideal physiques.

FOOD

- Type of eater: Omnivore—That's me. I'm a meat eater... vegetables and everything. Fish. It doesn't matter.
- Adventurous level: 9
- Taste preferences: sweet, savory

- Ethnicity: My dad is Nigerian. My mother is African and part Irish as well. I was born in Liverpool.

KVR: Do you attribute any of your tastes to your ethnicity and where you grew up, or something else?

MO: I've eaten Nigerian food from beef tongue to oxtail, fufu, garri, rice and all sorts of okra. Growing up, I'd also eat fish and chips and couronne. I grew up with friends who are East Indian (Punjabi), so I've had jalebi, roti and curry chicken. I've had friends who are Asian (Japanese and Chinese) so I've eaten authentic foods through them as well. I found it to be a very rich experience. Also, I've had friends who are Italian, Greek, Polish, from all over the world. I haven't shied away from any of their foods and I love it all. Thank God for diversity in friends. It's a good thing.

KVR: You've listed a lot of cuisines. Do you have any favorites?

MO: Boy, let me see. I love basic foods. Like when you talk about eggs, I could eat eggs every day. I'm absolutely cool with that. In fact, I remember when I was young, I had to feed myself and fill my stomach, but didn't have a lot of money. I'd buy the eggs and mix it with flour and get it really thick to add substance, so I'd cook eggs like that. It was great...You season it with a little bit of salt and pepper and eat it with toast and butter. You know, real basic stuff. I'd have it for lunch and dinner, but it works. It fills you and it tastes great. I'm really an egg freak. I think they're really healthy. Especially when you're living a healthy life. If you're into cardiovascular exercise and doing the right things, eggs are definitely complementary, natural and real. Your body knows what to do with real food.

KVR: Do you currently follow a certain type of diet, or meal plan?

MO: Not really. I think more than anything, I seem to have a schedule of not eating in the morning. I get out of the house, I'm at work early and I work through the afternoon. I have my biggest meal of the day usually around 2 or 3 o'clock. I work out and teach in the mornings and in the afternoons I have a couple hours downtime...I'll eat then. Then, I'm back up working again. Sometimes at night I'll have a little something...It's not really a supper, it's not that big. My wife will cook and she cooks really well—so I'll eat that, but I don't go crazy. I don't eat a lot.

KVR: I know you don't really eat in the mornings, but can you give me an example of typical meals you would eat during the day and the evening?

MO: Sure. Maybe I'll have a mixed salad, greens and tomatoes with a vinaigrette dressing. I'll have that with salmon and a little white rice. I don't have the biggest appetite. I love eating, but I also get kinda bored as well I have to say. The process of eating and putting the food in your mouth and chewing it all. I have a short attention span, so it's kinda hard for me to sit and eat a very big meal unless I'm around a lot of people. Also, I'm a very slow eater so that pisses my friends off when we go out for something to eat.

KVR: So, do you snack at all during the day?

MO: I don't really snack a lot. I mean, if I have a heavy client schedule then maybe I'll have a bag of mixed nuts that I'll grab in between sessions. Or, maybe I'll drink a latte. Sometimes in between sessions, I like to nibble on something really quick...like when I'm showing [students] how to do a jump rope maneuver, they'll jump rope so I'll grab a handful of mixed nuts or something like that and chew on them for a second.

When you start to get hungry, or when you're not eating right, you start to get light-headed, especially when you're working out at the kind of pace that we work out at. You want to make sure that you're not burning muscle and stuff you need. You want to have fuel in your body.

KVR: Are there any foods that you normally avoid, but crave...like "cheat day" foods?

MO: Ok, I love ice cream. I love Jell-O. When I fought, Jell-O used to be my ritual food. The first time I lost, I forgot to have Jell-O that day. I lost four times in my career and those four times I didn't have Jell-O. I know when you say "Jell-O" you think of Bill Cosby which kinda sucks now, but that was one of my ritual foods. And like I said, ice cream is amazing to me.

I think I kinda have a sweet tooth...I mean I definitely do. I'm a sugar freak. That's why I like anything that's sweet, like honey chicken or when my wife puts honey on salmon and bastes it a certain way. The first meal choice for me isn't necessarily salmon, but when she cooks it so well with the honey, I just can't say "no." It's sweet. Anything with sweetness on it, I'm gonna eat.

KVR: What are some of your all-time favorite foods?

MO: Fries would definitely be in there. Rice pudding would *definitely* be in there. Rice pudding for me...that dessert is the best. I love steak, but it would have to be really *really* juicy, like fall-off-the-bone kind of meat. Actually, I love ox-tail soup...it's just incredible. I like everything. I like mac 'n cheese. Let's see, what does the wife make? Everything she makes is so good.

I love chicken. I'm not a huge turkey eater because it feels like a lot of work to eat it and it also feels dry. Chicken usually has a lot more juice to it and I like that.

Oh, and bacon...I love bacon. I'm definitely a bacon eater as well. Maybe once every two weeks I'll have that, but again I just work out at such a rate that I tend to burn everything. I know ingredients are important as well and you have to pay attention to your caloric intake. But yeah, I do love some really good healthy bacon.

And I love salad. [My wife] does this skirt salad. It's like a pasta salad with lettuce, tomatoes, onions and all sorts of things in it and pasta with some mozzarella cut up in it. It's really good and it all melts inside and it just tastes really good. Because of my wife, I eat very balanced and very natural. We try to get as much from the market and Whole Foods as much as possible.

KVR: On the other side of things, what are some of your all-time least favorite foods?

MO: Ok, if it's hot...I can't do it so much. I could sweat doing anything, but if I'm sweating when I'm eating for some reason I'm uncomfortable. Hot food tends to take away the taste for me. All I feel is hot. I don't feel like I'm tasting a flavor...I feel like I'm experiencing heat and discomfort. I'll have haggis before I'll have anything hot. And

I sweat really easy...I like to sweat when I'm running and working out, but if I'm sitting and sweating at the table I'm just like "whoa." I just don't eat spicy stuff. Otherwise, I'm pretty adventurous with the exception of the heat thing. I'll try anything.

KVR: So you live in NYC right now, right? What are some of your favorite restaurants and why?

MO: Yeah, you know New York has an incredibly diverse food selection, restaurants and everything. Most of my food experiences have come from friends in their homes and not really restaurants. A lot of friends that I have, we tend to go to the same places like The Smith. We were in Little Italy for the San Gennaro Festival and had gnocchi and stuff like that. I want to try this Vietnamese restaurant that has pho and different things, but I don't really get out to eat a lot. I don't know...I'm kind of a confusing individual. I see myself going out a lot, but then I really don't when I think about it. Last month, we went out to Rice to Riches...I remember that, the rice pudding place. It was really great.

There's just so much diversity that it feels like I'm eating everyday food. It doesn't feel like I'm eating something that I wouldn't usually eat. It's just such a natural thing to walk into a different kind of restaurant and just order something that is not common. I was recently at an Iranian restaurant down in the 20s on the west side. I don't remember the name of it, but the food was great...that way it was prepared and the way it looked. You know, everything about it was amazing and something I tasted for the first time, but I don't remember the name of it. I couldn't tell anybody for my life, haha.

KVR: Do you have any favorite food & beverage products...things you usually buy when you go food shopping?

MO: [My wife and I] usually get coconut water or regular water. Every once in a while, we'll get sparkling apple cider. We make sure to get our grains in. We'll get bran, flakes granola...stuff like that. Those are constants. Eggs...They're from farm-raised hens and don't have any antibiotics. We're conscious of what we put in our bodies that way. We'll go to the butcher at Whole Foods. We usually have the meat cut up there in front of us. My wife goes to Chelsea Market. It's a really good fresh fish market. Yogurt is also a constant at the house...organic vanilla yogurt, for instance. Whole wheat bread, really good bread. Sometimes we'll go to Silver Moon Bakery and I'll get the peasant's bread. Sometimes just good bread and butter it's just like "yeah, that's all I need to eat."

Now that the boys are out of the house, we don't stock the place. Before, we would have it stocked. Now that they're gone, we can leave the fridge pretty much empty. We get fresh food, you know: tomatoes, cantaloupes, bananas, fresh fruits...all that kind of stuff. We don't buy the stuff that has the preservatives that lasts 2 or 3 weeks. It's the kind of stuff your body knows what to do with, it uses it for energy and gets rid of it. That's kind of how we roll now.

FITNESS

KVR: How would you describe your natural body type? Naturally lean, athletic, or stocky?

MO: I think naturally I'm very lean and thin. I don't build bulk easily. It's very hard for me. Aerobically, I'm always in a state of aerobic or anaerobic type of movement. As soon as my metabolism slows down, I'm back up and I'm exercising and teaching. So, my body reflects what I do. I don't teach anything slow and heavy, so I also won't gain size that way. Everything I do is very fast and long and you're always in a state of cardiovascular [fitness]. It burns a ton of calories and doesn't give you mass and keeps you very defined and sleek.

KVR: Do you have any go-to exercises or physical activities that you do?

MO: Yes, jump rope and shadow boxing, or hitting the bag...but jump rope is just incredible. I teach *all* the people that I work with (whether they're models or actors, it doesn't matter) I teach them all how to jump rope and to get really really efficient at it fast. You have to run for 30 minutes to equal the benefits of a 10-minute jump rope workout. Doing that kind of math...even I can do that. It's easy and the results and the benefits are just so fast. People don't want to spend a lot of time, they don't want to be bored and it helps you process food really fast and naturally.

KVR: At what point in your life were you happy with your overall fitness and reaching your fitness goals (however you would personally define that, whether it be physically or a state of feeling)?

MO: I think I've always felt, from the time I started boxing around 15 years of age, really comfortable and confident in myself physically. I actually played football before that, so really most of my life. I was always pretty confident in my "feeling," but not how I looked. When I got to my early and mid-20s, I really became comfortable in how I look and felt. To this day, I'm really comfortable in how I look, but I wish I had more energy, haha.

KVR: What keeps you motivated to maintain such a high level of fitness over all these years?

MO: I have a high level of expectancy of myself. Also, I know when people come to my classes, I've been around for such a long time now (since '91 on the fitness scene), people expect that of me. I like to practice what I preach and maintain that mental/physical balance. I really like the way it feels.

Like I said, when people come to class, they have that level of expectancy because they've heard about [my classes] for a long time...and they're experiencing it for the first time, so I don't want to let anybody down. So, it's kinda like a little bit of everything. It's never just one thing. Some of this, some of that.

KVR: You said you've been on the fitness scene since '91. Tell me a little about your journey.

MO: Yeah, I started with the first boxing fitness class in New York and kicked the whole thing off. I had retired in 1991 and then I started off in a little church in NYC. Then there was a place called "Crosby Street Studio" down Crosby Street in SoHo. From there, Equinox (when they *first* opened up) the Errico family asked me if I would come and teach there. So I did and it just grew from there. I used to do fitness festivals in Italy, Japan and Canada. They had never seen anything like Aerobox before.

I initially intended it as a cardiovascular exercise that men can do. That was my intent with it cause men would just go to the weights and lift the weights...That's it. Women were getting the cardiovascular and strength training. I was like, men gotta do that too, so that was my initial intent. It was boxing, shadow boxing, cardiovascular class, jump rope for men...but women took it over (they were like "yeah, this is cool") and just kinda blew it up. I trained guys for movies by Spike Lee and Michael Mann and got results, then models were coming and it was just blowing up. Now, all of a sudden there's this boxing thing all over the world and it's kinda cool. It's great cause a lot of boxers get employed too. We finally have something to do when we retire. It was a good thing all around.

KVR: Throughout these years of teaching, have you noticed that there is a certain type of student that tends to have a better result than others, or is it just anyone that does your workout routine has great results?

MO: Haha, that's interesting. I'd like to say that certain types of personalities, like A-type personalities tend to rise to the top. Dancers, for instance...dancers want to perfect everything. They're so good at emulating. They give you what you want and because they execute [movements] exactly the way they should, they're gonna get the most benefits. They're gonna sweat the most. They don't cut corners. They're used to giving the director the leg exactly at this degree, the arm at this degree, the hand movement, the jump...whatever it is. So they really go all out for you and their bodies are used to interpreting whatever you give them to interpret.

Even people who aren't athletes...there's a certain type of personality, people who have a psychological makeup and want to make everything perfect and isn't satisfied until they execute it and get it done. For my kind of class, that's what I've learned works best. Some friends have told me I should have gone into training competitive fighters because the way I teach people, when I get with them 1-on-1, the level of expectancy I have of them in class is really high. You know, I love people and I love teaching and I know everyone can get it. I teach people from kids to adults of all ages and everyone has different types of learning abilities and it all works. They all learn with patience and repetition. There's certain people who will get there faster, but we all get there.

KVR: Did you have anything else you want to add? Any tips on eating or fitness?

MO: Yeah, basically I guess my thing is, we don't do complex cooking...It's simple so the body can break things down. When I'm trying to accomplish something myself nutritionally, or body wise...again it's all about portion control.

I think every day we have to do aerobic exercise, not just 2 or 3 times [a week]. I don't think fitness is a luxury anymore because the foods we have are super (calorie-dense) foods...You could eat something the size of a meatball and it has like 100 calories now. It has ingredients in it that are not natural, but that's what the majority of us have to eat because not all of us have the luxury of being able to eat whole foods that cost more than manufactured stuff.

We have to be able to combat that and one of the ways we're able to combat that is really good aerobic exercise, cardiovascular-based exercise that will help our digestive system and help us process the foods (and even the drinks) that we're eating. We *have* to combat them. It's not a luxury anymore.

Our country, kids...everyone's getting more obese and it's just rampant now. The average body is not in shape anymore. It's not gonna get any better until we learn to: 1) control our appetite and 2) if you're going to eat that, you *have* to do this. Working out isn't a luxury anymore, like I was saying. When you go back a millennium or so, we used to hunt for our food and that's what working out is now; it's the hunt. So there's no need to eat if you're not physically putting out the effort. Everything's so convenient these days. When you're eating, usually you're eating because 1) you're bored or 2) you're stressed. Are we *really* hungry? We have to justify what we're eating.

Everything is there now. We don't need to put out the physical effort...everything's on your phone. You can text for your food to come to you. You don't even need to go downstairs to get your food anymore because they'll deliver to your door. We have to remember, we only have one body and you want that health to last as long as possible. One of the best ways we can do that is really good cardiovascular exercise...not the vanity type of exercises like curls and shrugs, that doesn't work. You need to do sports emulation kind of stuff. Do what a runner does. Do what a boxer does. Do what a ballerina does. Do what a basketball player does. We need to get out there. We need to move our bodies and exercise our minds...problem solved.

Andre Rush

Andre Rush a.k.a. "Chef Rush" is widely recognized as the strongest chef in the world. His 24-inch natural biceps are backed up by his ability to bench press 700 pounds and do 2,222 pushups a day (to bring awareness to veterans with post-traumatic stress disorder). As a 23-year military veteran, former Army Master Sergeant Rush had been granted the highest level of security clearance and has been a chef at the White House.

FOOD

- Type of eater: Omnivore—A lot of what I eat is chicken-based...I eat 4 whole chickens a day. I'm also a huge vegetable eater. I like to explore the vegan and vegetarian realm to make people think about what they're eating. Plenty of my dishes are plant-based. I eat a lot of fish as well. I'm all across the board.

- Adventurous level: "12"—I'm like Andrew Zimmern. I will try all kinds of things. I don't care what they are...That's part of who I am, especially being so well-traveled from Iran to Afghanistan and this place to that place. I've also eaten everything from animal brains and testicles to hearts and blood.

- Taste preferences: savory, spicy and sour (as a palate cleanser in between courses)

- Ethnicity: African American—I'm also from a small town in Columbus, Mississippi...very southern.

KVR: Do you attribute any of your tastes to your ethnicity is there something else in particular that you give credit to for your taste preferences?

AR: It actually started at a very young age with my curiosity of becoming a chef. I wanted to try anything and I ate a lot of everything.

Later on, different people whom I've met during my travels in Africa, Germany, India and many parts of Asia introduced me to different foods. The foods that people in the military would turn their noses up to were the foods that interested me the most.

KVR: What are your favorite cuisines?

AR: I love African and Asian...so many different types of Asian. I'm a sushi lover. When I order sushi or sashimi, I'll order a platter for six. I also love Indian food and Filipino food which can fall under the Asian category as well. There are so many types of Asian. That's a whole spectrum in itself.

I also love French. France has some of the best cuisine in the world as well as Germany...a lot of fattening food too, but they are one-bite delicacies which I do love. They are very complex with their flavor profiling. Then there's Italian. I'm getting so hungry just thinking about it. Of course I love southern food, which is my background, but of course it is also fattening.

Yeah, I like a lot of cuisines actually. I do. I'm not prejudice against any cuisine. If I could eat at 20 different restaurants with 20 different cuisines, I'd want to venture out and eat at each one. I'm very open and I didn't realize how open I am until talking to you, haha.

KVR: Do you currently follow a certain type of diet, meal plan, or pretty much eat whatever you want?

AR: That's a great question because I'm an endurance trainer. I'm in between a muscle bodybuilder and powerlifter. I lift 700 lbs, but as Arnold (Schwarzenegger) has pointed out, I don't have the big belly like powerlifters have. In endurance training, it kinda puts your body into survival mode. In survival mode, your body starts to eat all the muscle and it reserves the fat for later so you can survive longer.

Well, the way I train puts things in reverse so it will take away fat first because it thinks it needs the muscle to survive. I'll do heavy weights like 225 lbs or 315 for 25 reps or 50 reps at a time. Instead of doing light weights, I'll do heavy weights for a lot of reps.

Long story short, I eat a lot. The reason why I eat so much is because my body burns a lot. Even during a rest period, I can still burn up to 2,000-4,000 calories a day. That's just at an ordinary pace for me. When I go to the gym for about an hour, that's 2,000 more calories burned. I eat what I want to eat...high protein and very low carbs, which are complex carbs: brown pastas, wheat pastas and wild rice. I do a lot of edamame pasta and protein pastas. I do a lot of vegetables as well. I don't do sweets or desserts. I don't do sodas or anything like that. I do 2% milk. I make protein shakes myself with dehydrated peanut butter.

KVR: Do you have examples of typical dishes you'll have for breakfast, lunch and dinner?

AR: In an idealistic world, whenever I'm home long enough, I eat 24 hard-boiled eggs for breakfast. The thing is, I only eat 5 whole eggs and remove the yolks from the other 19 so it's just the whites. I know they say it doesn't hurt your cholesterol when you eat the yolks, but with the amount I eat, I'm not gonna wait to find out. I'll also do oatmeal, a protein shake, a wheat bagel, then I'll do some non-nitrate turkey (either half a pound or a pound) and coffee...all for breakfast.

Later in the day, I'll have a snack which is yogurt and a protein bar. For lunch, I'll have a whole chicken and I'll make it myself with some type of vegetable. After lunch, I'll do a protein shake. Then, an hour and a half later, I'll do another chicken and a half. Then I'll do a snack like some type of nuts. I'll usually have almonds with oatmeal; it's kinda like a fun little treat for me. I'll also add some peanut butter and either blueberries, raisins or a little bit of brown sugar. You can make all kinds of combinations. It's a perfect treat, believe it or not.

Then, I'll make myself a sandwich. I'll usually buy 8 pounds of salmon and smoke it in my smoker. I'll separate it into baggies and have it with a protein bagel each day. I do like to have it with a little bit of cream cheese and capers. That's another one of my little treats as well.

For the last full meal of the day, I'll have another chicken and a half, but I'll have it with some type of complex carb like a protein pasta, brown rice, or quinoa...love quinoa. Before the night is over, I'll have my dessert, which is milk with these protein clusters of oats and nuts all mixed together. I don't eat typical desserts or sweets, but that's what I'll do to finish the day off.

KVR: What are some foods that you would normally avoid, but crave...like "cheat day" foods?

AR: My cheat day food is hamburgers. I'm very picky though. I don't go to fast food places. I'll get a tenderloin and grind it up with all the fat. Those burger patties with only 20% fat or 8% fat—that's not gonna make a good burger. I'm sorry, it's not. Just render the fat and let it strain out, but keep the flavor profile. I would make two burgers at a time and they would be huge. I'd have them with sweet potato fries. I'll have my hamburgers with a big chunk of lettuce, huge tomatoes, extra pickles, ketchup, mustard...and that is a wrap. It's good as hell.

KVR: What are your all-time favorite foods? If you were to have a last meal, what would you have?

AR: If I had my last meal, I would do a global meal. It would be from everywhere. I would want my taste buds to go crazy, from sweet to sour to savory to umami...I am such a foodie as far as eating different things. When I think "all-time favorite foods" though, I don't know. I eat so many different types of food and make them in so many different ways.

The thing is, food brings back memories. I grew up with southern food, so maybe I'd have a nice southern meal...with a side of Asian food, Italian food and everything else.

KVR: What are your all-time least favorite foods?

AR: That's a tough one. There's not really any food I don't eat, but the last time I remember not liking something I ate, I think the cook just didn't make it right. It didn't have the right flavor.

So, my answer would be...bland food. Food with no love.

KVR: I know you said you don't really eat out, but do you have any favorite restaurants?

AR: No, I don't have any favorites because I cook so much. I did do a television shoot at a steakhouse that was called Kilinger's, I think. I went there and talked to the staff. They were so hospitable and customer service was so great. The general manager asked me to sit down and have a meal and they presented me with a smorgasbord with all the food. I have to tell you that the food was great, but even if it was just mediocre, it would have tasted a thousand times better because of the level of service and attention to detail.

KVR: When you go grocery shopping, are there any foods or beverages that you'll usually get?

AR: Well, the thing I always get is chicken. I'm always gonna get chicken, at least 3-4 gallons of milk, a case of eggs (that's 120-150 eggs), cereal, fresh vegetables and then a huge container of quinoa. That's my foundation right there.

I always boil my eggs because I like to eat 100% of the eggs. When you scramble eggs, you have to crack them and it can leave a bit of membrane in the shell. Also, when I boil eggs, I can eat them like candy. I can eat 5 to 8 eggs in no time...I just pop them in mouth like nothing. If I were to make them scrambled, it would take forever to eat. There's a method to my madness.

KVR: When did you actually begin your career as a chef?

AR: I was actually a cook back in '93-'94. I'm naturally very competitive, so back then, it was like an insult to me when people called me a cook. It's funny because I remember someone posting my picture on social media and someone else commenting, "Hey, wasn't he the cook for the superintendent?" I usually don't say anything, but

I was like, "NO. I am not the cook for the superintendent." I had to hold my composure, but it is what it is.

People don't understand, but I'm proud of what I've accomplished to become who I am today. I recently got 150 letters from a group of kids I visited at a school. I had my chef's jacket on and they thought I was a superhero. They were pointing to me saying "I want to be a chef. I want to be a chef bodybuilder." It's very humbling. I'm a role model now and I have to act as such. So yeah, it all started back in '93-'94 when I started cooking and my skills grew from there.

KVR: What inspired you to become a chef?

AR: My mom inspired me to become a chef. After church or Thanksgiving (for instance), my mom would make these huge, huge meals for all of us. Now, my family and I saw each other all the time. But when my mom would cook, we would congregate around the table, sit down and pray. It was like a whole different family. Food brings me joy and good memories, especially my mom's meatloaf and potatoes.

I used to cook with my mom when I was younger. I used to taste the food and play with it. My dad was a very brawny man and was all about work-work-work-work-work. My little side-gig between working was cooking with my mom and I really enjoyed it.

KVR: How did you end up becoming a chef at the White House?

AR: Working my ass off, haha. Long story short, back in 1997 I was a young kid and I was working at The Pentagon for the Chairman of the Joint Chief of Staff, General Shelton. It was another high profile job and I was extremely driven. I had 3-4 catering jobs at one time and I had a clearance, which was very important to have. Clearance isn't the reason why I got into the White House, but it is necessary to get a job here in D.C. One of my mentors (who was 17 years my senior) who was working in the White House saw how hard I was working and invited me to come over and interview, so I did. They liked me and I came back periodically while staying with my job in the military and running my own catering business as well. That just carried out through all these years.

KVR: How demanding is it to cook for the President?

AR: As demanding as breathing, haha. It is what it is. You know with the White House, you have your teams over there. The primary chef was there every day. I was not always there because I was pretty busy with multiple jobs and my work was very demanding. For instance, sometimes I would be in Africa helping refugees building houses, so I couldn't be around the White House all the time.

The White House kitchen is actually quite small; remember it was built in the 1800s. It's a small place. They weren't thinking about the kitchen when they were building the White House.

My point is you need the right kind of people that you trust to be part of your team. It doesn't matter if you're the greatest chef in the world. If you don't have that cohesion to be able to follow and lead, you're not going to be a success; you're not going to have a successful team. That's why I've stayed around for so long.

I'm not the best chef in the world, but I'm what one of the best chefs in the world would want to be. You can't mess up. You don't get second chances. You get no second chances whatsoever, so it has to be perfect every time. When I say "perfect," it really is scrutinized to perfection which is a great thing. Everyone has to be on the same page, in the same league and make each meal like it's the last meal they would ever do.

KVR: Does the President decide everything that he wants you to cook for him, or are you given leeway to cook what you want?

AR: The duties are divided up between the people who work there. I've done this for a very long time, not just in the White House, but for other principals as well. Nine times out of ten, we will take guidance from whoever the principal is, so the food will be something that he prefers.

People have to remember that when the President goes to different countries and different events, they're eating all the time. You're eating what the other host is serving you. When you do come into your own abode, you want to have something that you prefer.

KVR: What are some of your absolute favorite things to cook?

AR: Believe it or not, 97% of the meals I do are not repeats. I am that person. I have to challenge myself. I have to challenge my mind. Even with chicken...If I cooked chicken a million times, 999,000 different times, I'd make it a different way. It's kind of like the Forrest Gump deal with the shrimp. I literally do everything different all the time.

I use cooking as therapy for those in the military with PTSD. I'll go out food shopping and grab stuff, without any rhyme or reason and I'll give it to them and go, "Make me something." They're minds just go beserk-o. There's no recipe. It's not scripted. No measurements or anything. It's the worst part about it, but it's also the greatest thing about it. Five minutes into it, they're minds start clicking and putting things together. It's like they go into survival mode.

Generally speaking, it's a lot more impactful on men because men have that arrogance to them. It's a challenge and a sport. Then, as they get better at cooking, they start bringing their skills home to their family and it brings them closer together. It combats the part of their mind affected by depression and anxiety caused by PTSD.

If you didn't know, I do have PTSD myself. My coping mechanism for that is the same as how I help others, through cooking. When I'm cooking solo, I will go to the farmer's market and make up the menu as I'm picking out stuff. That's why I almost never repeat what I cook. Some people use art, bodybuilding (which I also do myself), or something else; but what everybody has to do every day is eat.

FITNESS

KVR: How would you describe your natural body type? Naturally lean, athletic, stocky or a combination?

AR: I wouldn't say stocky. Even at 300 pounds I wasn't stocky. I'm not lean. If I had to choose between ectomorph (lean & long), mesomorph (muscular) or endomorph (high tendency to store body fat); I would say I'm a mix of endo-meso.

KVR: So you've been called "The Strongest Chef in the Military" and "The World's Strongest Chef." Was that an image you created over the years, or just a byproduct of the way you lived your life?

AR: That's the truth. I did not craft that image. It's funny because I used to do a lot of different things and do a lot of demos so people used to be impressed with my size even back in the day. I have been lifting weights for a long time and it's only recently that I've gotten some real public attention. I did an interview with Rx Muscle and Dave Palumbo where we touched on that.

When I started lifting 500, 600 and 700 pounds, people in the military would say "he's the strongest chef in the military" because nobody else was doing what I was doing. Because I'm a chef, it seems more impactful. As more people have found out about me and say that I'm the strongest chef, I've accepted it and said "Ok, yes...I am the strongest chef."

KVR: Do you have any go-to exercises? I know you do 2,222 pushups a day and can lift 700 pounds.

AR: The 2,222 pushups is not even considered an exercise for me. I do get the physical benefits from them, but the pushups are for a cause for suicide awareness and suicide prevention. Twenty-two vets a day commit suicide. Instead of doing twenty-two pushups a day, which doesn't sound like a lot, I do 2,222 pushups because it's more impactful.

The push-ups only take about an hour to an hour and fifteen minutes if I'm lackadaisical about it. If I'm busy, it can take up to 3 or 4 hours since I'll knock out 500 pushups (120-150 pushups at a time) in between my tasks. It doesn't take long for me because my body's used to it. I had a bunch of Marines tell me they were going to do 2,222 pushups a day also and I said, "NO. Do not do it. Take baby steps. You should start out with a hundred and work yourself up." If you just start doing 2,222 pushups, you're going to hurt yourself. It's a process.

My actual workouts include activation of my legs. People always ask me how they can grow. I say legs are the tree trunks of the body. You never see a big tree with a small trunk. The wider the trunk, the bigger the tree is gonna grow. Strength training for your legs can also further stimulate testosterone growth. I love arm workouts, of course. You can get so much depth and growth out of them because you can control them more.

These are just some arm workouts that I do, which I shared with Men's Fitness:

- seated curls: 5 sets of 25 reps for each arm, 5 sets of 25 reps both arms
- forearm rope pulls: 5 sets of 25 pulls for each arm
- seated incline curls: 4 sets of 15 reps

- one arm cable curls: drop set starting at 72 pounds

I love every aspect of the body. I tend to focus on my back, arms, legs, chest and "boulder shoulders" as I call them. If I don't have time and I want to get a workout in, I always workout my back and arms, then a shocker with my legs...all with heavy lifting. Yes, I can lift 700 pounds. That's a bench, not a deadlift. A 700-pound deadlift wouldn't be impressive for me.

KVR: At what point were you happy with your overall fitness?

AR: I've never been happy with my overall fitness. I say that because I see these guys at Mr. Olympia and the Arnold Classic and I see their dedication; they live in that world 24 hours a day. When Kate Bennett took that picture of me at the White House that went viral, I hadn't been to the gym for three months. I thought I had looked like crap, but I have muscle memory. You know, a lot of people make excuses about working out and I get angry sometimes because of my muscle memory, which takes a million times longer to show growth than if you just train from the beginning. So when I do work out, my workouts have to be more impactful. I've never in my entire life had a phase when I worked out, let's say, four months straight. I've never been able to because of work, because of this, or because of that.

I've never taken steroids or enhancements, which has been a big topic with everybody from YouTubers to internet trolls. I think I'm an expert on steroids now because people ask me about it all the time. It's funny because not that long ago, I saw Nick's Strength and Power on YouTube and they said I was #natty. I was thinking, "I don't even know what the hell 'natty' means." I guess it means "natural," so I guess #natty...that's me. It's part of my lifestyle. People can do whatever they want to do. I don't care...To each person their own. But, I would never encourage any kids to do any kind of drugs, steroids, or anything like that.

I've never utilized my full potential, so I'm going to buckle down and try to be the best me ever over the next year. I consider myself an alien, so my strength right now is probably better than 90% of men, even without working out full-time. I am very blessed for that. I'm fortunate.

KVR: How long did it take for you to get to the size you are now?

AR: When I was younger, I was smaller and built for speed. When I was in high school, they wanted me to play football, which I was good at as well. They had a little gym upstairs. So I went to that gym not knowing what to do, but would go there periodically in the summer to work out for football. In a few weeks, I was full of muscles. I was able to bench press 315 at 13-years-old. Everyone was like, "What the hell? What did you do?" Back then, no one (including myself) even knew what steroids were so that wasn't even a question. Long story short, I could work out for a little bit and my body would respond tremendously. As I got older and bigger, I was able to tweak my workouts and make the results last a lot longer, retain that muscle memory.

I've always been bigger than the next person, but it's taken about a decade of hard work and heavy lifting to get to my current size, the 260-300 pound range. That is a long time because I haven't been working out consistently. Gaining the right knowledge, however, takes longer than that. That's 15+ years of knowledge and training hundreds of people (I'm a fighter as well) that goes into the process of getting to where I am today.

KVR: What keeps you motivated to maintain such a high level of fitness?

AR: It's an extreme amount of work, especially when you're trying to help the whole world. That being said, helping everyone actually keeps me at that level now. I do work out for my health, but I know that whoever that one person is (whether it's a kid, woman, or someone else) that is inspired by what I do makes all the effort worth it.

I remember someone on LinkedIn had messaged me saying "Chef, I wasn't gonna go to the gym today, but I saw your post and you made me go to the gym. You're my motivation." I would hear these comments over and over and over again. That is what inspires me. That's what drives me. That's what makes me say, "Ok, I love doing this now."

There's a guy that had been going to my gym for about ten years and his body had never changed because he didn't know what he was doing. He would go to the gym just to go to the gym. I ended up training him and his body immediately responded because he was finally doing what he was supposed to be doing. His muscles were properly getting stimulated. Along with my own health and longevity, everybody inspires me to keep doing what I'm doing wholeheartedly.

KVR: Any other tips or advice regarding health, fitness or eating?

AR: My only other advice is: "knowledge is power" and "you are your greatest asset or your worst enemy."

It's you against you. A lot of people talk themselves out of doing something beneficial when it should be themselves talking themselves into it. I shouldn't have to be the person that tells you to do something, or inspires you. Unfortunately, that's the way it is sometimes. Look, I get it. I feed off of other people as well, which is why I'm here...but ultimately it comes down to you. When you're on the right path, just keep doing what you're doing. Never quit. Never waver. Never give up. Never stop.

PERSPECTIVE

NOOO! I DON'T WANNA GO!!! I DON'T WANNA!!! AAAH!!!
AAAAHH!!!

The ear-splitting wails of a teary-eyed, red-faced child echo through the chamber. A steady flow of mucus drips from his nose. His cries intensify as he is dragged away. Choking between sobs, the young boy fights with all the might he can muster in his tiny body, kicking and screaming to avoid being forced out into the world of craziness.

What kind of cruel, merciless person would torture a poor child like this? His mom. And what God-forsaken place would allow such an atrocity? Disneyland. Or, more specifically, Candy Palace. This is just an ordinary day for the average tantrum-throwing toddler who isn't getting what he wants. Sadly, it is such a common occurrence that the majority of passersby simply took a glance in the direction of the ruckus, then went on with their business. A few others, presumably parents who have recently endured a similar scenario, watch wistfully and sympathize with the exasperated mother who simply wanted to pick up a souvenir for her sister.

What causes young children to practically lose their minds in relatively innocuous situations? Without delving into child psychology, one major reason is that they lack perspective. Toddlers have been alive only for a few years. Long-term memory doesn't normally kick in until *after* the age of two, so they have little to no experience on which to base their actions (and reactions). Instead, they act on what they feel and want inside a sliver of a moment known as "now." They aren't thinking that the giant piece of candy they want is full of bacteria-attracting sugar, which can lead to cavities if they don't brush their teeth properly, or that they might have had a treat earlier in the day and that a sugar-heavy diet can lead to more serious health issues. They have no concept of monetary value—that anything with a widely known cartoon character on it costs a multiple of the price of similar generic candy—or of how hard their parents might be working to afford quality meals to nourish their children's growing bodies. All toddlers know is that if they want something, they must have it. If they don't, they act like the whole world is coming to an end. Of course, many parents know that their child's unreasonable behavior stems from a limited point of view. "It's a small world after all." *Ba-dum tss!* As a catalyst for appropriate action, having perspective is incredibly important on multiple levels.

Remember my encounter with the mind-blowingly delicious cinnamon roll back in the first chapter? If that brief glimpse into my food life was the one and only thing you knew about me, you'd probably think I was an obsessed sugar fiend and quickly label me as someone who either has or is on the way to developing type 2 diabetes. In reality, that couldn't be further from the truth. The story that opens the book was a dramatized depiction of me eating something I eat less than 0.001% of the time, an insignificant iota. I eat a wide variety of foods and indulge in cinnamon rolls at the annual county fair only because those freshly baked, baby-soft rolls really are as tempting as I've portrayed. I don't even go at it alone. Have you seen the massive size of those cinnamon rolls at your local county or state fair? To make it more manageable, I'll split the roll evenly with whomever I'm with. After a few bites, I'll wash down the inevitable sugar build up in the back of my throat with some water. It takes about a bottle of water for me to finish my half and cleanse my palate of that lingering saccharine aftertaste. Once I'm done eating, to feel less bloated and to avoid the onset of a food coma, I'll go for a light stroll.

There is way more to eating smart than solely focusing on *what* you eat. Factors like the frequency of eating a particular food, the amount of that food you eat in one sitting, the other foods and beverages consumed around the same time and regular physical activity all come into play as well. To quickly recap my previous example, I treat myself to a cinnamon roll of that caliber once in a blue moon. *And* I eat only half of it. *And* I immediately dilute everything I've eaten by drinking a bottle of water. *And* I keep my body moving. And one more thing: my next meal is bound to be light and healthy, including a fulfilling lean protein and lots of vegetables. That doesn't sound nearly as bad for your health as eating a giant sweet roll straight up, does it? You can apply these adjustments to anything generally considered "bad food."

Actually, there is no such thing as "bad food," only bad practices. Unless you have a food-related allergy or other medical condition, you really can eat anything you want if you're responsible about how you do it. If you're not used to this sort of process, it may seem like a lot to keep track of when all you want to do is eat. But do I consciously think about doing these things as I'm eating? Not a chance. For me, having to monitor all my actions takes the fun out of eating. So, how do I remember to follow little tips like these every time I eat? I don't...at least not consciously. It's second nature to me so it feels effortless.

What I *do* pay close attention to is how I'm feeling. If I'm feeling any sort of discomfort, I automatically react in a way that I know will make me feel better. If I'm hungry, I eat. If I'm thirsty, I drink water. If I'm starting to feel full, I stop eating and walk it off. I don't ignore how I'm feeling because that exacerbates things. If you don't eat when you're hungry, you'll eventually feel like you're starving and tend to eat more than your body needs. If you don't drink water when you're thirsty, you might resort to whatever beverage is available to you when you're absolutely parched, even if it's a sugar-packed soda. If you don't stop eating at the first sign of feeling full, you might eat till you feel like you're going to burst and succumb to a food coma. (Eating massive amounts of food and sleeping afterward is a regular practice for sumo wrestlers to gain weight. Unless you're looking to pack on the pounds, it's ill-advised.) If you don't follow an indulgent snack with something healthy for your next meal, you'll feel lethargic. And you probably won't get in any exercise.

Because I've constantly tinkered with and practically mastered my personal eating habits over the years, I know what I need to do to feel my best. Anyone can do this, but you must train yourself to make tiny good decisions that work for your lifestyle and your body every day (with the guidance of your medical professional, of course). It adds up. Over time, it will be—pardon the pun—a piece of cake, and you will have significantly improved the trajectory of your overall health.

If you're wondering whether you should limit your "guilty pleasures" to once in a blue moon, the short answer is "no." The caveat is, once again, that you need to figure out what works for you—what is sustainable for your personality and lifestyle. For me, what works best is treating myself to a bit of indulgence (usually some form of dark chocolate) every day. That way, I never feel deprived or get uncontrollable cravings. At the same time, I generally eat healthful meals and snacks that leave me satisfied, yet light and energetic. So, when I do end up having that molten chocolate lava cake or silky smooth crème brûlée, I'm in a total state of happiness and am left with zero eater's remorse.

Cakes are healthy too; you just eat a small slice.

-Mary Berry

People commonly believe that those who love food frequently overeat, which does ring true for many. However, *because* I love food with such great fervor and because I savor each and every bite, I rarely ever go overboard. In the case of the cinnamon roll, the introductory bite is practically pure ecstasy. I take my time chewing and tasting the complementary flavors to thoroughly process and prolong the enjoyment with each mouthful. The incredible sweetness means it takes only a few bites for me to have my fill. I don't even feel the need to have a full stomach because my taste buds have had enough. Why would I want to keep eating if it's no longer fun?

In economics, this drop in gratification is explained by a fundamental principle called "the law of diminishing returns." In layman's terms, it means that the value you get from something decreases after a certain point. As you have likely experienced, when you dig into a massive feast after not eating all day, the first few bites are almost always the most pleasurable because of the prior buildup of hunger and anticipation. Barring any hoity-toity dining etiquette, the speed and level of intensity at which you devour your food is normally the highest in the first few minutes and tapers off as you approach satiation.

You can witness this first-hand on an extreme level at the hot dog eating contest held every 4th of July in Coney Island. This contest features some of the greatest competitive eaters in the world who train their bodies year-round to consume gargantuan amounts of food in a short span of time. For context, most of us eat one, two or *maybe* three hot dogs in one sitting. In 2018, Joey "Jaws" Chestnut set the world record at 74. Even these trained professionals cannot always maintain the speed and intensity they exhibit right out of the gate. Why? We all (except for those with binge-eating disorders) have limits, so we either get full or get tired of eating. When we near our state of satiation, eating becomes less and less pleasurable—no matter what the dish. Instead, it leads to ever-increasing feelings of discomfort, forcing us to stop eating. So, unless you're going for the next competitive eating title, slow down and enjoy your food.

Perspective around food and eating is also important as it relates to experiencing different cuisines. I am always looking to expand my horizons with food. The world has so much more to offer than the typical western fare of pizza, burgers and tacos (although each one of these foods is a world in itself).

After graduating from college, two of my best friends and I made it a point to eat together at least once a week at a new-to-us restaurant serving an authentic cuisine we had never tried before. Most of the time, these were mom-and-pop hole in the wall restaurants offering some of the most intensely flavored dishes I had ever tasted. It was eye-opening to learn of the existence of so many different cuisines and so many different dishes within each cuisine. For example, when the average American thinks of Japanese food, what usually comes to mind? Probably sushi and teriyaki. Maybe ramen. Americanized versions of these dishes have been served in the United States over the decades, so Americans got used them. Those who are well-traveled or seek out restaurants known for authentic cuisine know that there are tons of other popular types of foods in Japan, such as *donburi, okonomiyaki, omurice, soba, sukiyaki, takoyaki, yakiniku, yakitori* and many others. Opening ourselves up to these different cuisines and dishes within each cuisine provides perspective that there are an infinite number of delicious foods out there. (Luckily, the influx of immigrants to America over time and, more recently, the widespread exposure of different foods on the internet has also led to an overall improvement in the diversity of available cuisines.)

Eating your fruits and vegetables as well as other healthful foods can be incredibly easy when they're prepared in an endless number of mouthwatering ways. And just when you think you've tried every cuisine there is to try in the world, you can break them down further into regions and sub-regions to experience all the variations of that cuisine. Also, new food creations seem to pop up every day. The world of food is limitless. Don't get yourself in a rut eating the same stuff over and over. Not only can eating the same foods day in and day out get mundane and monotonous, but it could also multiply the effects of whatever nutrients those foods are lacking or any harmful ingredients that might be included. If you're an absolute creature of habit and actually like eating the same things every day, just be sure to take the extra effort to make sure you're providing your body with what it needs. For everyone else, diversity in foods FTW—that's "for the win" for you non-gamers.

Gaining a well-rounded perception of fitness is important as well. It can be quite daunting to think that in order to maintain your optimum health, you must work out regularly *for-ev-er*. However, you must also breathe approximately 23,040 breaths a day and blink approximately 28,800 times a day for the rest of your life. In addition, over the course of an average human lifespan, you will spend approximately the equivalent of 26 straight years sleeping and more than four straight years eating. All of these activities can seem overwhelming when you look at the raw numbers. Yet it would be absurd to think they're not worth doing, because they're essential.

Fitness is essential, too, if you want to live a healthy life. You just need to put things into perspective and think of exercise in terms that are feasible for you, whether it's 30 minutes of activity every day or two hours of activity every few days. You'll have more success staying fit if you remain open to trying different activities until you find something that you can see yourself doing on a regular basis, something that becomes as routine as breathing and blinking. Because there is no one way of getting the physical activity needed to keep your body healthy, it's a great idea to engage in multiple activities so, just as with food, you don't fall into a rut. If you like to spend time outdoors, you could base activities on the season. You could ski, snowboard or sled in the winter; hike, run or bike in the spring and fall; and swim, snorkel or paddleboard in the summer. If you like group activities, you could join a local recreational sports team or sign up for a class at your local gym. If you prefer one-on-one attention, hire a personal trainer or coach so you can receive direct guidance and a workout plan tailored specifically to you. If you like to listen to music and dance, then dance! Find a form you enjoy, whether it's hip-hop, salsa, tap, ballroom, break, shuffle…the list goes on. Best of all, you can dance pretty much anywhere: at a class, at a club or in the privacy of your own home.

These represent just a tiny sliver of all the different activities that could get your fitness up to par. Just as all the individuals featured in this book have found activities that work for them, you can find something that works for you. It all depends on your interests, lifestyle and personality. In the same way the world of food is limitless, so is the world of fitness. Go and explore the possibilities.

Keeping the big picture in mind is imperative. We are humans, not machines. (Well, the great majority of us who aren't full of bionic parts and aren't controlled by AI are human, but that's a completely different story.) Don't give yourself a hard time for having a "cheat day" or two regarding food or missing a few days of working out. That's normal and to be expected. All you have to do is get back into your usual healthy routine and move forward. The worst thing you could do is throw your hands up in defeat and fall back on old bad habits. The longer you stick with bad habits, the harder they will be to break. Know that with the necessary determination, you can always return to your correct path and restart your new, good habits.

Finally, always look to broaden your perspective by expanding your knowledge about and experiences with food and fitness. Nobody knows everything. Check your ego and recognize that there is always more to learn. As you build a greater understanding, you will most likely end up taking the most appropriate and most enjoyable course of action for you...unlike the tantrum-throwing toddler in the "happiest place on Earth."

Blake Horton

Blake Horton is the founder of "The Blake Diet." He is an extreme intermittent faster and eats 3000-4000+ calories a day while staying in shape. His counterintuitive methods and controversial claims are supported by his healthy vital signs, which were taken and shared on Dr. Oz. Since 2013, he has helped thousands of people lose weight.

FOOD

- Type of eater: Omnivore—I eat a wide variety of things. I do eat meat. I love fish. A lot of my meals happen to be vegetarian, but mostly my cereal and dessert meals. It really depends on what I'm in the mood for.

- Adventurous level: 10
- Taste preferences: savory and sweet, savory being the more dominant preference
- Ethnicity: African American and Italian

KVR: Do you attribute any of your taste preferences to your ethnicity, or is there something else that you give credit to for your tastes?

BH: I attribute my tastes to a mix of imagination. I think about what flavors would work well together. A lot of times people will think, "Well, bananas can't go well with chicken...that certain foods can't go with certain foods." I've mixed so many crazy foods together, which the flavors pair very well, and people would love them given a blind taste test. But, if I told them *what* foods they're eating together, they wouldn't like it.

For example, cheese sauce and syrup are two things I tend to mix together in foods. Chicken and bananas are something I've done many times. Peanut butter and jam on burgers go extremely well...That's another great sweet and savory example right there. I do these "banana dogs" which are bananas in an Italian roll that kinda looks like a hot dog...I top them with jam, peanut butter and even bacon. So, all kinds of things.

129

KVR: What are your favorite cuisines?

BH: I guess you can call it Italian food, but anyone from Italy would say it's Italian-American. I do a lot of stuff with pasta and Italian rolls. I've done fettuccine alfredo in bread, penne vodka in bread, spaghetti in bread, lasagna in bread...all types of pastas. I also love pizza, but who doesn't love pizza?

KVR: As an extreme intermittent faster who typically eats only eats once a day, what does a typical eating and drinking schedule for you look like?

BH: I drink many fluids throughout the day (mostly water and sometimes coffee and energy drinks). I don't do dry fasting. Some people do dry fasting where they basically dehydrate themselves throughout the day; I believe you should stay hydrated. I just go about my day. I work 14 hours or more a day, sitting in front of my computer for most of my day and I'm super busy. I usually take a break from work late afternoon and go for a bike ride, but sometimes the gym (fasted).

To get back to your question, I usually do everything I have to do for the day and before bed, and the last thing I would do is my meal...my giant meal, which is almost always after midnight (about 95% of the time). I'm usually super busy until about 11 p.m. and by the time I make dinner, I usually end up eating after midnight. I like to eat when I can relax and enjoy my food. Keep in mind, I film and do recipe videos. I do live streaming for members of The Blake Diet so I have to set up cameras and lighting and go over the nutrients and ingredients live with my clients in addition to cooking. I have to do so much prep before I actually get to eat. Regardless, to do one giant meal midday and go about your day, you're kinda looking for acid reflux, heartburn, indigestion and maybe not feeling so well...in my personal opinion. Especially with the amount of food I consume in a day, if I did it *all* in one midday meal, I wouldn't want to do anything after that besides nap. The body's meant to digest the bulk of its food while resting.

KVR: Do you curb your hunger during the day by drinking?

BH: No. Actually, the less frequently you eat, the less hungry you get. It's very counterintuitive, but when you eat once a day you just no longer get hungry...ever. It's friggin' awesome. It's the coolest thing ever. I know when to eat and I know how many calories and nutrients I need to eat. When I'm making a meal, then I get in the mood to eat. I'm not physically hungry, but the mental hunger kicks in. True physical hunger doesn't really happen until a few days with no food, or an extreme caloric deficit.

Most people in America will never actually have to experience true physical hunger. However, they'll experience mental hunger (where your mind and body play games with each other), which is the realest thing in the world. You think you're zapped for energy and think, "I just need to eat." Your stomach may be growling, but it doesn't necessarily mean you're hungry. People just always think they're hungry and need to eat. But once they adjust to one meal a day or eat in a shorter period of time, like just lunch and dinner, they'll be less hungry than when they eat all day. Once you start eating for the day especially when you spike your insulin, you're gonna want to eat the rest of the day. So, I always recommend starting your eating later in the day rather than starting the day off with a meal and eating through your [allotted] calories all day.

KVR: How did you get the idea to eat like this? Why did you decide to do it?

BH: I lost 60 pounds when I was about 30 years old. I started by doing "Bro Dieting," the small meals spread out throughout the day thing which got old quickly. I was eating out of Tupperware and the whole meal prep thing and that sucks...that just friggin' sucks. When I was doing that, I was hungry all the time, watching the clock and waiting for my next tiny meal. When it was time to eat, I'd scarf down my meal in literally two minutes. I mean, the meals get so small when you break them up into 5 meals a day with protein shakes and snacks. As soon as my tiny Tupperware meal was over, I'd be looking at the clock going, "When's the next time I'm going to eat?" I was just miserable and hungry all the time. Plus, my social life took a big hit at the beginning of my weight loss journey because when you eat small meals spread throughout the day, by the time my friends wanted to go out or there was an event going on, I'd be almost out of calories. I would usually not even go out because I was taking the weight loss thing so seriously and didn't want to ruin my progress.

I remembered reading about intermittent fasting and started doing my research. There were a few crazy random people who were saying (well, I thought they were crazy at the time because I thought it was bullshit)...but they were saying, "This actually works." I didn't follow anybody's program because a lot of the programs didn't make complete sense to me. I just found some common themes and I did things my own way. I transitioned super slowly and carefully because I was scared that I was gonna get fat eating all these carbs before bed. I was scared I was gonna lose muscle if I went all day without eating. So, I *really* transitioned slowly and was very careful and diligent and kinda treated it as a science experiment. Then I took it to a whole new extreme. I didn't know anyone who was eating one meal a day at a time, but I went with the same principles. I was like, "Calories control body weight and health & well-being come from getting the proper nutrients. I don't see why this wouldn't work." There's less dishes and more time for me to do other stuff. Now, five years later I'm here.

When I started reading about intermittent fasting, I was into bodybuilding forums at the time. I was really into weight training, which I'm not really into so much right now. I was just reading a lot about the "rules" of what you need to do to build the best physique. There were some people in various forums who mentioned intermittent fasting saying, "You know, this works too." I kept seeing [intermittent fasting] pop up randomly, but not a lot at all. Now it's more popular than it's ever been, but it wasn't popular at all the time. It was a rare occurrence, but I was intrigued enough cause I was like, "If I get to eat like a fat-ass and continue to lose weight and make body composition progress...if this works I'm down 100%." I was so sick of always being hungry and eating small unsatisfying meals that it was worth the risk to me! I no longer get hungry. I'm more than satisfied with my meals. It all sounded too good to be true, but it's worked.

KVR: How long did it take for you to adjust to this form of intermittent fasting?

BH: Me, personally, like I said I did it slowly and gradually. I went from eating five meals a day (shakes and snacks) to two meals in a matter of a month or so. Then I did two meals for a while and ended up doing one meal many months later just out of pure convenience because I didn't have time. I was just so busy. I was like, "Let me see if I can just pack this all into one meal." *That's* how the one meal thing got started.

KVR: Do you take any days off from your diet?

BH: Well, when you say to me, "do you take any days off from your diet" I say "no" because The Blake Diet is very flexible so it's easy to stay on track. But if you ask me "Do you take any days off from the conventional rules of intermittent fasting?" I'll say, "Absolutely." Most people just have these rigid rules for intermittent fasting and they can't go to social events or weddings if it falls outside their eating window. I don't teach that. That's why I created The Blake Diet with a member's website & community where I teach people how to do intermittent fasting in the best, most flexible way possible. If I want to eat two meals for some reason, of course I do. If I want to eat at a different time, of course I do. I teach my clients how to do all types of things like, "Hey if you want to eat brunch on Sunday, here's how you do it... Here's how to set it up and still reach your goals." So yes, I guess you could say I take plenty of days off from intermittent fasting in the conventional sense, or according to conventional rules but again The Blake Diet has different rules.

KVR: What are some examples of a typical meal that you'd have?

BH: Giant pizza slices are many times covered with mac 'n cheese or spaghetti. Giant donuts. Now let me be clear when I say this…All of my meals, I scientifically make them fit my nutrients. They look very unhealthy, yet they fit my daily nutrients. A lot of people just think I eat junk food. The meals that look like they're really high in sugar are not *that* high in sugar. People will say, "I can see the grease and the fat," but the meals I make are not super fatty or greasy at all. People just jump to all these conclusions. Don't assume you know what I'm eating. I'm like a mad scientist in the kitchen. I weigh all my food. I get healthier ingredients and lower calorie stuff. I make everything super colorful. I eat about 15 pounds of fruits and veggies a week, but nobody sees it because people are attracted to the cheese sauce, peanut butter and the regular carbs like bread and pasta. So yeah, giant pizzas, giant donuts, giant gyros and giant tacos. My favorite things to make are giant foods.

KVR: Are there any foods you normally avoid, but crave?

BH: None. Anything I want, I figure out how to make it and make it fit my nutrients. Even if I eat out, there's no real "cheat foods." The worst that happens is that it fits my calories, but not my exact nutrients...which is not a big deal at all when only eating out about twice a week.

KVR: What are your all-time favorite foods? If you were to have a last meal what would that include?

BH: As I said, different pizzas are among my favorites...even dessert pizzas. I'm known for making Fruity Pebbles pizza. That's pretty wild. People love my cereal meals. I love cereal cause it's nostalgic when you eat the old school cereals that you used to eat as a kid. I make dessert sandwiches a lot, like the "banana dogs" with peanut butter, jam and cookie dough. Oh, and pancakes and waffles. I love breakfast foods, like platters of giant pancakes. I use regular pancake mix with my own concoctions to make them higher in protein. What else? ...Pasta subs. All kinds of pasta in a sub.

KVR: What are some of your all-time least favorite foods?

BH: I hate whole wheat and whole grain stuff. I'm not a fan. I think it's like chewing sandpaper. Whole wheat pasta, whole wheat bread, whole grain pretty much anything...I'm just so not a fan of. I'd rather get those nutrients elsewhere. The whole reason why people eat whole wheat and whole grain is because they think it's better for weight loss...not everybody, but 99% of people. Once that myth is busted, they want their white bread, white pasta and white rice back. Also, grilled chicken. I'm not a fan of grilled chicken cause it's so dry. I'm not saying you can't take chicken breast and make it juicy, grilled chicken just gives me the idea of being so *so* dry.

KVR: Do you eat out at restaurants at all?

BH: I do restaurant promotions a lot of times. We do the most epic restaurant meals, my girlfriend and I. However, I know how to make that work and still make progress with my diet. So we absolutely eat out. Even on my members' site, I have a "how to set up a New York-style pizzeria night for dieting success" tutorial. I have a "how to get drunk while losing fat" tutorial. If it's a late-night restaurant promo, we do our whole day's worth of food in one meal but there are some days when I have a scheduled restaurant promo during the day or early in the evening and on those days I'll usually split my nutrients up into 2 meals, doing the second meal right before bed. The Blake Diet is set up for people who want to enjoy life and be fit and healthy, but not be so serious...cause people have lives. We're on this earth for a very long time and people are just making themselves miserable with these bullshit diets, which are so restricting. People are scared of things for no good reason. They're doing stuff that doesn't matter and the stuff that matters, they're not doing. I help people get their lives back. Yes, you can go out and eat. Yes, you can get wasted. My girlfriend and I and pretty much get drunk on Instagram every weekend while live streaming. Some of the live streams I don't even want to watch cause I'm like, "oh man, this is bad."

I don't know if you saw, I was on Dr. Oz and he revealed my health. Everybody was so pissed off that I was healthy. Rather than learning specifically about my diet, signing up for my program, seeing what's there and going through the tutorials; most people get so angry. It's because, like I said, they've been doing the stuff that doesn't matter, making themselves miserable and getting it all wrong. Then they see me eating giant pizza slices and it just trips a fuse. They're like, "This is bullshit. You're still not healthy. I don't buy this." I've gotten so much hate from that show. It's awesome though...It's great for business. The new members are loving the diet!

KVR: When you actually do eat out what are some of your favorite restaurants and why?

BH: It's hard to say my favorite restaurants because it's almost always a restaurant promotion when I do eat out. Alright, let's just be general. I love pizza after a fun night of drinking and partying. Almost every Saturday night, my girlfriend and I do pizza. We'll usually do take-out. Sushi...I love sushi. I actually had someone make me an 8.5-pound sushi roll (with some cooked meat, not ALL raw fish). That was pretty cool and I ate the whole thing. I would say, if I eat out, I do like steak and lobster. Lobster rolls are great. Burgers are cool, but not those extreme burgers with ten patties stacked on top of each other (unless I make my own healthy version). Oh, I love empanadas. I love gyros. I love New Jersey diners...They have disco fries (cheese and gravy on fries), mozzarella sticks and a wide variety of foods. Whenever I eat out, unless it's pizza, I'm usually ordering or given the widest array of things, so I basically get to eat a bunch of things.

All of the meals you see me make, I wouldn't want to eat at a restaurant because not only would it be way outside my calories, but it would be so greasy and fatty that it wouldn't be delicious and I would get sick of it pretty quickly. When I make my own meals, I usually make one main thing and a side. I calculate the nutrients of my own foods. But yeah, eating out...let's say pizza, sushi, steak and lobster, empanadas and gyros.

KVR: Do you have any favorite food or beverage products you like to get when you're grocery shopping?

BH: Most of my meals will include French or Italian bread. If not, there's probably pancakes or waffles. If there's no pancakes or waffles, then there's pasta or rice almost every friggin' time. Those are my staples. I come up with my idea for my meal first, then it ends up on bread or cooked in dough or something like that…Whatever I can fit into my calories without throwing my nutrients off.

FITNESS

KVR: How would you describe your natural body type?

BH: I was naturally lean and ate like shit for a couple years. I put on 50-60 pounds in two years when I went from two active jobs to one desk job. I was expending way less calories but not consuming any less. I didn't know what a calorie was at the time. I just didn't care. I had a girlfriend at the time and was settling down, about to turn 30. I was like, "I'm done. It doesn't matter how fat I get." I was just having fun with it. Then, I got dumped by her. I was single and turning 30, so all of a sudden I cared that I was fat. That's what started this whole thing. I'm so glad she dumped me.

KVR: How often do you work out and for how long?

BH: I don't have a regimen or schedule. I'm probably gonna be in the minority in this book. My thing is knowing how to eat accordingly with how much you worked out, or how much you didn't. I could work out 2 hours one day and not at all the next day and half an hour another day. It's really easy for me to manage that because I usually don't eat until the end of my day. I basically estimate my energy expenditure and it's like, "Alright, so I can eat 3500 calories today...or I can eat 4000 calories today." Depending on what I did or did not do, then I'll eat accordingly.

I work out roughly 6 days a week. As far as the types of training, I go to the gym twice a week for about 45 minutes. I have a lot of fun on my BMX bikes (and while I personally don't look at training as fun, it expends calories so I should mention it) Between bikes & gym, I work out half an hour a day to 2 hours a day...It's so random. If life gets in the way and I'm gonna go do something else and not work out, or I'm stuck working in front of the computer and I don't get the time to train, I just know how to eat accordingly. It makes it so much easier than thinking, "Oh, I *have* to go to the gym for this long so I don't lose my progress."

KVR: At what point were you happy with your overall fitness? How long did it take?

BH: I was happy with my physique when I lost 60 pounds in maybe 7 months...8 months. I was really happy with my physique. I went from fat to fit and super shredded. I was on cloud nine about my physique. However, the happiness kinda fades when you're a slave to the gym, in my opinion. I was very happy with the food, but I wasn't purely happy with my lifestyle at the time. I was spending all my free time in the gym. That happiness came as I figured out how to eat smarter and not work out harder.

Let me say this, happiness is not about the physique. Happiness came when I figured out how to get my life back and enjoy food and alcohol and a social life while having the physique I wanted. There's just so many people who are a slave to the gym, a slave to their diet and posting this stuff online...putting up this front that they're super happy cause they're shredded and they look awesome, but they're miserable inside. Given the opportunity, they would take their old life back when they used to have fun.

KVR: What keeps you motivated to maintain such a high level of fitness?

BH: I do stuff I enjoy. I have all these BMX bikes. I do wheelies. I enjoy bike riding a lot. I ride in the park and different places and I hang out with a crew of 14-year-olds half the time cause we all have the same bikes...I'm serious. I do fun stuff. I'd say 20% of it is more physique-related, but a lot of it is doing fun fitness stuff I enjoy. That's changed many times, but right now it's BMX bikes. It doesn't matter what's gonna get your body composition results the fastest if you hate it, because it's not sustainable. I just don't want to go to the gym a lot so I make slower progress building muscle but progress is progress. I

143

literally don't have the attention span when I could be outside on my bike having fun.

KVR: Are there any other go-to physical activities you like to do besides BMX riding?

BH: My giant BMX bikes are the most fun. That's really what I enjoy right now. It's been calisthenics at one point. I was into handstands and all types of crazy stuff with jumps and whatnot. Bar stuff (where you're flipping over bars) and doing gymnastics-related calisthenics...It changes all the time and I just do what I like. They used to call me "Spiderman" at my old gym because I would scale the wall to the top deck. I would run up the wall and grab onto the bottom of the top deck and climb up. I'd do all kinds of crazy crap like that. I would go to the gym, but I'd be so bored of weights that I'd have to do something different. I just like a challenge and the adrenaline rush more than anything else.

KVR: Anything else you'd like to add?

BH: Life is very, very long. You have to enjoy your food, because if you're not enjoying your food, it's gonna be even longer. When you hate your diet, every minute is gonna seem like a year.

Melanie Iglesias

Melanie Iglesias is a quadruple threat in the entertainment industry. She's a model, TV & internet personality, comedian and R&B/pop singer-songwriter. Voted Maxim's Hometown Hotties winner in 2010, Melanie has since appeared on Guy Code, Girl Code and the World Poker Tour. She has also performed stand-up comedy and has released multiple singles from her EP "Context."

FOOD

- Type of eater: Pollotarian—I eat a lot of chicken...and carbs and vegetables. I eat a lot of chicken breast. I'm kind of finicky with stuff like that to be honest.

- Adventurous level: 5—I stick to what I like.

- Taste preferences: savory, salty, sweet and spicy—I just started getting into spicy foods this past year. It's pretty new for me. I told you I'm a "5" on the [adventurous] scale. Spicy foods are something I realized is something I really do appreciate if done the right way.

- Ethnicity: I'm Puerto Rican and Italian. I did an ancestry test and it was pretty surprising to find out that we are not Filipino in the slightest. Somebody somewhere told us some wrong information. My dad is Italian and my mom is Puerto Rican.

KVR: Do you attribute any of your taste preferences to your ethnicity, or is there something else that you give credit to for your tastes?

MI: I'm really big on Italian food and Puerto Rican food because I grew up with it, but I think I would love it even if I wasn't raised with it because it's just delicious to me. I eat a lot of pasta, breads, cheeses, prosciutto and paninis. That's me all day.

KVR: Besides Italian and Puerto Rican, what are some of your other favorite cuisines?

MI: Yeah, I really love Thai food. I love Thai curries and spices. It's something that I've gotten into lately. I also love a lot of Greek food and Chinese food. I'm from New York, so I love Chinese food—New York-style Chinese food. It's very different from other Chinese food I've realized, moving to LA especially.

Yeah, so I really love Italian food, Greek food, Thai food, Mexican food and Puerto Rican food. I like some Indian food too. I've really been getting into curry lately. I love rice, anything with rice. Rice is my favorite. I could eat rice with every meal. In the morning, I'll eat eggs over medium over white rice. I'll also eat any sort of fried rice, yellow rice like Puerto Rican rice...just all sorts of rice.

Oh, and I like soul food. I really like soul food...like southern food.

KVR: As an entertainer, I imagine there's a lot of pressure to maintain a certain image. Do you follow a certain diet or meal plan, or do you pretty much eat what you want?

MI: I think everybody is different. What works for me is not gonna work for the next person. Personally, I don't believe in depriving yourself. I think life is too short...eat the cake. On the other hand, a part of my job is about maintaining a certain image, but I really don't try to let that control or dictate what I'm eating because I want to be happy. Food is a big part, I think, of personal happiness. If you eat good, you feel good. Sometimes you're having a bad day and you just want a bowl of fried chicken. I think that's ok, but you can't eat like that every single day. For me, I'll have weeks where I'm eating super healthy...like less carbs, more protein and salads. Other weeks I'm like, "You know what, I'm just not gonna think about it this week." It just depends on what's going on [with my schedule]. I really try not to deprive myself.

KVR: Can you give me an example of typical meals you'd eat throughout the day for breakfast, lunch and dinner?

MI: For breakfast, I'll usually have two boiled eggs and then I'll have an English muffin, some bacon and maybe some yogurt. For lunch, I'd probably do a sandwich, but I'll eat it sometime during the daytime. I try not to eat too many carbs late at night. Then at night, I'll probably have some form of chicken with a vegetable, like a chicken piccata with sautéed broccoli, or something like that. I eat something similar to that every single day.

KVR: Do you have any go-to snacks?

MI: I'm a big snacker. I love it all. I love all sorts of pastries, cannolis (I love Italian pastries), cookies...The thing is, you have to tell yourself, "Ok, after three I'm putting it away." You can have it and taste it.

I think that when you don't eat it and you finally get to, let's say you've been dieting super hard for weeks and then you finally get that taste when you hit your cheat day, then you just go crazy and you end up overeating. I think if you just let yourself have things in moderation, your body doesn't crave it as much and you don't end up overdoing it or hating yourself for it. That's how you go down the rabbit hole.

I know a lot of people who do keto and when they finally start eating carbs again they just kinda go crazy and put [the weight] back on. I don't really believe in that. I don't like all those big diets and fad diets. You just have to monitor yourself. There are these apps that tell you how many calories you're eating, but then you end up getting obsessed with those things too.

You just have to eat slowly and when you're full (or getting there), just stop. Try eating dinner with somebody else and make conversation so you're eating a little slower. Before you know it, you're full and you didn't overdo it.

KVR: What are some of your all-time favorite foods? If you were to have a last meal, what foods would you want to include?

MI: My last meal would be either be McDonald's or Taco Bell. It would probably be 13 taco supremes or something *if* it was the last [meal], like "Ok, this is how I want to die...just eating taco supremes." I read somewhere that Nicole Richie eats Taco Bell. She's pretty fit and her trainer lets her eat Taco Bell once a week because he also realizes how important it is to not deprive yourself. That way you don't go binge eating because you haven't had it in so long. So, I don't see anything wrong with that. And McDonald's...I love the chicken nuggets. I used to eat a lot more fast food when I was younger, but I'm getting older now and learning a lot more about eating healthy. But if it was a last meal situation, I'm going for either one of those two things.

One of my all-time favorite foods is pernil. My mom makes pernil, Puerto Rican pork. If you haven't ever had that, it's gonna change your life. If you like pork...*whoo*! It's delicious. I'll eat that and I'll eat bacon, but that's where I stop with pork.

KVR: What are some of your all-time least favorite foods?

MI: I don't eat seafood because I'm allergic to shellfish. Beyond that, I just don't like the way fish smells. I can't enjoy food if I don't like the way it smells. I don't know how to describe it. The smell just turns me off on fish and I just don't find it appetizing, so I tend to avoid it. I haven't had a piece of fish since I was a kid.

When it comes to lobster and crab, I psyched myself out. Yeah, I'm allergic. You know the movie *Hitch* with Will Smith when he gets the allergies on his face? That's kind of what happens to me. My tongue will swell up, my face will get swollen, hives everywhere...I get all swollen everywhere. I remember washing dishes once when my dad just finished eating some shrimp and I had hives all over my hands. It's a pretty dangerous allergy for me. I think that kinda made me a little bit paranoid when it comes to seafood, so I just avoid all of it. Beyond that, I just really don't like the way it smells so I don't eat it.

KVR: What are some of your favorite restaurants and why?

MI: That's a tough question. I used to work at this place in New York called Cipriani. That place has great Italian food. There's one in Miami too...It's delicious. It's probably one of my favorite restaurants to go to when I'm back home.

There's a place in Brooklyn called Pies and Thighs. They have this thing called the chicken biscuit. It's my favorite thing in the whole world to go eat when I'm back in Brooklyn.

Then there's L&B's pizza in Brooklyn, which I grew up on. They're famous for their Sicilian pies.

KVR: Do you have any favorite food or beverage products?

MI: I like different fruit drinks. I still drink Capri-Sun. My sister and I make homemade iced tea. We'll go and buy a bunch of tea and we'll make our own sweet tea at home. It's better than McDonald's sweet tea. When I'm at home, I'll just drink different iced teas or lemonade.

I love fresh lemonade. I love Martinelli's apple juice. Martinelli's is a must-have.

As far as food, I love to get creative in the kitchen. I like making things like stuffed artichokes, so I actually buy that pretty often. I like stuffing it with different things every time I make it. Sometimes I'll make a stuffing that has mushrooms in it, or I'll add different cheeses. I like to play with that kind of stuff. I love making vegetables taste delicious. So I buy a lot of vegetables at the supermarket and I'll come home and make zucchini fries or stuff like that. I also buy a lot of chicken breasts and just do different things with chicken because that's mainly how I get my protein. I have a bunch of friends that will come over a lot, so I'll do chicken tacos (which are easy to make), or just a lot of things that are easy to put out and share. It looks cute and doesn't take a lot of effort.

FITNESS

KVR: How would you describe your natural body type: lean, athletic, curvy, etc.?

MI: I'm naturally lean. My family and I...we're pretty lucky in that sense. But I know if I'm not careful, like anybody else, I will gain a little bit of weight.

I'm naturally pretty thin and pretty lean...and I guess the majority of [my family] is pretty lean. I still exercise a lot. I love doing cardio. I love doing a lot of walking, running and playing sports. So, I don't know if it's because of genetics or we're all just naturally athletic. We're all pretty thin or lean or muscular, but we all play sports and exercise a lot. I'm not sure how much genetics plays a role in that.

KVR: How often do you work out?

MI: I do some form of cardio every single day—at least 45 minutes to an hour, whether it's walking, hiking, playing some sort of sport, playing with my dog or going on a run. I would say a couple times a week, I'm doing 5-minute abs or I'm doing yoga. I'm watching YouTube videos and taking out my yoga mat and I'm just doing some exercises in the house.

The thing is, I don't like the gym. The gym makes me very uncomfortable for some reason. I don't know how to use the equipment and I'm too shy to ask for help. What works for me is just going on YouTube and finding somebody who can really explain the exercises and what they're doing with objects you already have in the house. I like stuff like that. I get anxiety at the gym because I'm comparing myself to everybody else who has been there way longer than me...That's not a good feeling. I just always feel like everybody looks like they know what they're doing, but maybe they don't. Maybe I just think that they do, but I always get in my head at the gym.

Instead, I like to work out at home or play volleyball or play handball or I'll run around the basketball court or go swimming. Swimming is amazing cause it's a full-body workout. I love dancing. I'll turn on music and dance for 45 minutes in my house. I'll clean the house in my high heels so that my legs get a workout...I'm not joking. I learned that from my mother. We'll be in our pajamas and have our high heels on at home while cleaning. It really works though. As long as you're staying active and keeping your body moving, it doesn't matter where you do it. Don't sit down too long. Sitting down is so bad for you. If you're sitting down all day, you have to make time to keep your body active cause things will stop working, or bones will start cracking. I like to make sure I'm stretching every single day. That's another thing I do—I stretch a lot. First thing when I wake up, the first 30 minutes, I'm stretching.

KVR: At what point in your life were you happy with your overall fitness?

MI: I think, "Is anybody ever *really* happy with their fitness?" I think we can always find somewhere to improve. It really just have to come from a place within, doing it for yourself and not doing it for other people. I know I had to go on hiatus from Instagram for a few months because I felt like I kept comparing myself to other people with pictures that are photoshopped or airbrushed...or even if they're not, girls who live at the gym and have amazing bodies.

You know, we're not all meant to have the same body type. It's just important to do what you can for your body type and just remember, we're not all meant to have the same waistline or the same measurements. Every single body is different. I started realizing that only now.

I just entered my 30s and I just started feeling very confident in myself at this age. Had I known that I would be this confident right now, I might have done a lot of things differently when I was younger. I used to think, "Maybe I should get this done, or maybe I should get that done." Then you get older and wiser and think, "Wow, I'm confident now." I think that comes with age, just learning and speaking with people. When you talk to people and realize they have the same insecurities as you, even though you may think they look amazing and perfect it's like, "Ok, we all kinda feel like this." We all get a little insecure, so don't obsess over the things that you can't change. Just do what works for you and don't aspire to look like anybody else because it's just not realistic. We're not made of the same stuff...We don't have the same DNA, so just be the best version of yourself.

It took a long time to realize that. I think you'll always look in the mirror and find something that you want to change. The more people I talk to, the more I realize most people want to change something on themselves. I think talking to more people about that and opening up with friends and being vulnerable and speaking honestly about that makes you realize, "Oh, you know what, I'm good. Even this person's not happy and they have the body that I want."

As you get older you look back at pictures of yourself and think, "Wait a minute, I looked good back then. Why was I so insecure?" It's sad, almost, when you think about all the missed opportunities when you could have been enjoying yourself and living your life and not thinking of certain things. It's just a part of being human. One day, we're all gonna be old people and we're all gonna be like, "Did we enjoy our lives?" You're gonna look back on it and wonder what you've spent your time thinking about or focusing on. I think that's something you're not gonna want to look back on, thinking about all the times that you could have been enjoying yourself but didn't cause you were too busy criticizing yourself.

I've even seen women who give birth and hate their bodies afterwards. I'm just like, "Your body just did something amazing. You are a goddess. You just pushed out another human being." Some people may look at stretch marks and think of it as a negative thing, but I think we should wear these things like badges of honor. This is what makes us unique. These flaws are what make us...us. I think we all just need to be a little easier on ourselves and enjoy life a little bit more. Food is something fundamental that we need to survive and we need to eat and is fuel, but it's also something that can give us great pleasure. So, we should not be depriving ourselves and comparing ourselves to other people. Just do everything in moderation and enjoy your life and don't get carried away, but have a good time.

KVR: What has kept you motivated to maintain such a high level of fitness?

MI: I'd say it comes with the territory of being an entertainer. I also just need to be physically fit. I'm an asthmatic so the better shape that I'm in, the less asthma I get. I need to always be doing some form of cardio because it helps me breathe a little better. That motivates me a lot. I just want to live a long, great life. Someday, I hope to have kids, so I want to be in shape...and that doesn't necessarily mean a certain weight, but that I want to be healthy overall. The things that I do extend to my overall health. I'm just really motivated by that. I want to be healthy and I want to be around. I want to have the stamina and endurance to entertain for a while.

Caroline Labouchere

Caroline Labouchere is an international model who began modeling in her 50s. She is known for promoting ageless beauty, running ultra marathons, breaking age barriers in the modeling & fashion industries while empowering women to be their best selves. She has had campaigns in British Vogue, Tatler, Hello and White Magazine.

FOOD

- Type of eater: Omnivore—I eat pretty much whatever I want to eat. However, we (my husband and I) are more herbivore than we have been and are becoming more so.
- Adventurous level: 2—I'm not really adventurous at all.

- Taste preferences: it varies...salty (after I go on a run) and sweets (on the weekends)
- Ethnicity: English, Italian and Austrian

KVR: Do you attribute any of your tastes to your ethnicity and where you grew up, or something else?

CL: My husband was in the army for 30 years, so we've traveled a lot. We lived in India, Canada, America, Germany and Dubai...so my tastes developed from the traveling. I love spicy food. But my tastes don't really have much to do with my breeding. It's more of my experiences and travels.

KVR: What are your favorite cuisines?

CL: Indian is my favorite. However my go-to is pizza, thin, very thin and crispy. Quattro Formaggi.

KVR: Do you follow a certain diet or meal plan...or do you pretty much eat whatever you want?

CL: Eating has to be a lifestyle, something you can stick to. For me, it's no sugar and no carbs during the week. Then, I can have all the fun stuff during the weekend. Generally, I don't drink alcohol, but I will have an occasional glass of good champagne.

KVR: Can you give me an example of a typical dish you'll have for breakfast, lunch and dinner?

CL: I've never eaten breakfast. I probably don't really eat until lunchtime. For lunch, I'll usually have almonds or some cheese. Then at about 6 p.m., I'll have a green shake which is protein powder, kale, cucumber, no fruit (I don't eat any fruit) and celery (I love celery). If I have made a vegetable chili or something yummy in my slow cooker, I eat that without the carbs that I cook for my husband.

I've gone through phases of snacks. Now it's almonds, but I went through quite a few months of eating salted popcorn. Also, I went through a period of eating eggs all day. My weekend treats are Maltesers. They're like Whoppers, but much nicer. I run for about 2 hours on Fridays, so I figure I've offset the "naughty stuff" a little.

Many people practice intermittent fasting and really, without a deliberate plan, that's what I do.

KVR: What are some of your all-time favorite foods?

CL: I do love Chateaubriand with a Béarnaise sauce. I rarely have a steak these days, but I would if I was where I knew it was going to be amazing...with French fries. If it's just me and I've had a really hard, long run, I might cook myself a cheese and potato pie. This is layers of different cheeses and potato, salt, pepper and filled to the brim with milk. It's cooked until it's golden brown. I have to eat it by myself because I eat it out of the dish. I don't share. My mom used to make it and it's a huge treat.

KVR: What are your all-time least favorite foods?

CL: Offal. I cannot bear it. My parents used to try to make me eat liver as a child and I had to sit at the table for hours in front of that plate.

KVR: Living in multiple different countries, what are some of your favorite restaurants you've been to?

CL: David (my husband) and I don't go out much. Having said that, we love Akira Back and Masti. Hugely creative and delicious.

The Arts Club is a favourite. I first went with the owner of the Club. You can imagine we had pretty much everything on the menu. I love to pick rather than eat one large serving. It was pure overindulgence. The Arts Club in London was phenomenal. Soon to open in Dubai.

Our all-time best place to take visitors is Ravi (Pakistani) which serves great food in Satwa. It's absolutely authentic. Bottles of soft drinks no cups and melamine plates. Fast, fresh and cheap.

I can't really think of anywhere else. We really go to bed early because we both exercise a lot. David is out of the house by 5 a.m. most mornings cycling or running or swimming because he's an Ironman. So we're pretty much in bed by 9:30 p.m. which makes it not really easy for going out for dinner. We're morning people.

KVR: When you go grocery shopping, do you have any favorite food or beverages that you'll often get?

CL: Avocados. We LOVE avocados. I could eat tricolore any day of the week…That's a mozzarella, tomato and avocado salad. To die for, but it only tastes nice if you have nice tasting products. The food is not fabulously tasty here in Dubai because food has to travel a long way and ripening is not a natural process.

KVR: Throughout your life, how have your eating habits evolved? Have they changed greatly or remained pretty constant?

CL: My eating habits are relatively constant. Even when I went to school, I didn't eat breakfast. As we don't have children in the house anymore we don't have biscuits and cake out at tea time. I suspect there are similar phases in everybody's life. Now, it's back to just the two of us so we can do what we want. I'm free to be what I might have been originally. You just get to a stage in life and think, "Maybe this is the real me." You don't have your mother, you don't have children.

It's just us. So sometimes I don't have an evening meal during the week. That's probably the biggest change. I still have to cook an evening meal for my husband, which I do, but I don't always eat it. We still sit down together and I drink my shake while he eats his supper. So throughout the week I'm just snacking and drinking shakes. I don't get hungry because I am used to this regime. I think anybody can do anything they want to do if they just make that decision to do it. What is important to you? The breakfast thing has never been an issue. Lunch (not being a daily meal) has just come over time, but it's just me. If my husband's home maybe I'll have some cheese while he has some soup and cheese on toast or biscuits or something. But, I don't feel the need to eat a meal.

FITNESS

KVR: How would you describe your natural body type? Are you naturally lean, athletic, curvy or some combination?

CL: I'm definitely not curvy. The last time I was curvy was probably when I was sixteen. You know when you go on the pill for the first time, you tend to put on weight, big boobs and muffin tops. Well, I was in Italy at the time for three months and I ate a lot of pasta. I was not happy. I guess happiness has a lot to do with how much you eat too. I came back after three months and my mother was horrified. I hadn't really noticed it because it wasn't important to me at the time.

I would say I have good genes. My mother is small. She doesn't eat a lot. She's by herself now and I guess it's harder to eat when you're alone. At the opposite end are the brunches in Dubai. Brunches are *huge* in Dubai. Everybody says "It's the "Dubai stone. You put on the Dubai stone." (Note: 1 stone = 14 lbs = 6.35 kg) Everyone goes to brunch on Friday...a lot of people and a lot of food. We go very rarely. I think we've been to four in ten years!

KVR: Do you have any go-to exercises or physical activities that you do regularly?

CL: I run every day. David actually trains me. If he (as my husband) told me what to do, I probably wouldn't do it...cause he's my husband. But, he uses TrainingPeaks, which is how he can watch all the people he trains and make sure they're all doing what they are told. So, every day I get an email from TrainingPeaks telling me what I have to do. Because it's an email, I feel like TrainingPeaks is telling me what I have to do, so I do it to the letter. You either get graded green, red or amber depending on how you worked out. So, there's accountability because nobody wants a red or an amber.

I love goals. If you're not sure, don't make it too tough. Don't go out for a run. Go out for a walk-run. Perhaps run to a lamppost then walk to a lamppost. That's good enough. That's all you have to do. It's what you can sustain and what works for you. Consistency is the most important thing.

KVR: At what point were you happy with your overall fitness?

CL: Umm, are you ever happy? If I enter a race, I have to be faster than my previous time. There's no point in me entering a race unless I try to beat the time I did before. So, I decided I wasn't going to run any marathons or half marathons because I didn't want to run fast anymore and I felt too much pressure. So, I thought, "Ok, I'll do an ultra." I had signed up for the ultra in Cape Town which is 56 kilometers (34.8 miles). "I'll just do an ultra so I can just go 'chug chug chug chug chug.'" It's going to be hard, but I'm going to do it. I'll even walk-run if I have to, but I'm just gonna do it. Then when I entered I found I had to run a marathon to qualify.....aargh. So, I signed up for the Dubai marathon. I got my time to qualify even though it is a soulless and hot marathon.

KVR: Is there anything in particular that you've changed in your fitness routine as you've gotten older?

CL: I should make more changes but I am quite habitual. I went through a yoga phase, but I'm not there in my life right now. I know I should do it and I watch people bending over double and think, "Ohh, I really, really should be doing that." I've gone through a phase of doing a little bit of Pilates. I try to roll regularly, but I'm really, really slack. I have just started playing tennis again after ten years and I'm loving it. At my age I ought to weight train regularly once a week, I'm adding that in from now on.

I stand on one leg when I'm boiling the kettle or brushing my teeth because balance and stability is incredibly important. Regularly before our runs, we stand on one leg with our eyes closed for 20 seconds on each leg. Also, we squat with our heels on the ground. Good runners develop a good squat and the stability to balance. That's part of my daily routine. As people get older, they tend to fall and are more fragile. Once you fall, you're off to the hospital and that's when things can start to go wrong.

KVR: What keeps you motivated to keep such a high level of fitness throughout all these years?

CL: I think I'm motivated now by not wanting to give up and join a club of 50-year-olds that are still living (possibly) in the last century. I strongly believe that fifty is the new thirty and that we are probably going to live to a hundred. My grandmother was 97 when she died. So, I live with the assumption that I'm going to live to a hundred. My husband also thinks he's going to live to be one hundred years old. (He's going to be the oldest Ironman ever, apparently.) If we both believe strongly enough, I'm sure it will happen.

We're much younger in mind and body now than we were. Someone sent me a message saying "Wow, you're wearing Converse shoes. I'm 42. I didn't know I could still wear Converse. But they look so good on you, so I'm going to start wearing them." I thought, "Hang on, you're only 42!" Your age only depends on your mindset. Someone else messaged me saying, "I'm 50-something. I'm divorced. I'm really unhappy and I'm looking really old." You have to make a decision, don't you? You can do something about it. How are you going to be satisfied with yourself? What can you do to change that? It's 2019, you can do pretty much anything you want now. Life is too short to be unhappy. Be a Viking, not a victim.

KVR: What does aging gracefully mean to you?

CL: It means being happy with myself and being the best self I think I can be. So, if it means having Botox in my chin...If it means doing something like that, I'm going to do it. There's just so much talk about "be happy with your wrinkles" and that's fine if you're truly happy.

But, I don't particularly want to get wrinkly and have that really saggy face. For me, it's about not changing myself. I don't want to change my face. I don't want a different nose or anything major. If there's something small I can do to make myself look and feel better when I look in the mirror, then I'm likely to do it.

I have a few quick tips. I don't think you have to pay a lot of money for products. Apple cider vinegar works as a toner. Coconut oil is a great moisturiser. Certain generic brand names can be just as good in a Vitamin C serum. I use hair and nail supplements because my nails just don't grow, but I found the cheaper ones are just as good as the more expensive ones. A lot of Googling of reviews is always good.

KVR: Do you have any other tips on eating, health or fitness?

CL: Yes, you've just got to create a lifestyle that works for you. A lot of people say they're looking forward to indulging themselves over the holidays. You don't have to indulge yourself for a week or two. You could just do it day-on day-off. Or maybe two days of indulgence and two days of being good. Just don't do it continually because you'll have to pay for it in the end. A routine is great if you can stick to it. It has to be something you can live with. Remember, consistency is key.

Brandi Mallory

Brandi Mallory is a motivational speaker who is an advocate for plus-sized women. She was featured on ABC's television show Extreme Weight Loss and is a long-term success story, losing nearly 200 pounds. She has kept the excess weight off over the years through dedication and healthy lifestyle changes.

FOOD

- Type of eater: Vegan & Vegetarian—I'll also have salmon and shrimp, but not very often.
- Adventurous level: 7—The most adventurous things I've had are alligators and frogs legs, stuff like that.

- Taste preferences: Savory, but I do like the mix of sweet and salty sometimes and I like the mix of sweet and savory.
- Ethnicity: Italian and Black

KVR: Do you attribute any of your taste preferences to your ethnicity, or is there something else that you give credit to for your tastes?

BM: I attribute *everything* to my ethnicity...Ethnicity and environment. I would include environment as well because I grew up in a very diverse area and went to a very diverse high school, so I had so many different friends from different cultures and I've tried so many different things because of that.

KVR: What are some of your favorite cuisines?

BM: Mexican is definitely my favorite. Italian would be my #2. I'd go with American after that.

KVR: Do you follow a certain diet, meal plan, avoid certain foods, or pretty much eat what you want?

BM: I carb cycle, so that's pretty much the extent of what I do right now. That means, no carbs for my last meal each day because that's when you're winding down and not burning as much. Instead, you'd replace the carbs with a healthy fat. Say, for example, someone normally has a piece of salmon, mashed potatoes and broccoli for dinner. For me, I would take the mashed potatoes out (I'd still have the salmon and broccoli) and I would do a salad with it and put avocados on it...something with a healthy fat. Or, my dressing would be a full-fat dressing so I'm getting that fat intake. I'll also put almonds with some vinaigrette in my salad, something like that. For my body type, I have to stay on top of that part.

I don't eat meat, so no red meats of course. I try to stay away from anything that's been alive, minus plants. I do eat cheese still...That's why I can't completely call myself a vegan, because I still eat cheese, I still eat sour cream. Outside of that, I don't really do too much dairy. I do eat eggs. I also eat every fruit and vegetable you can think of. If you threw it at me, I would tell you, "yes."

I really don't know what this diet would be called, but my meal plan is centered around no dairy (for the most part), no meat and all types of carbs. I work out so much that I have to have carbs for all the calories I'm burning. I gotta have that energy.

Also, I try to eat my last meal at a reasonable time. I do have one day a week when I'm out late teaching back-to-back dance classes, so that is the only day I eat late, because I don't finish until 10 p.m. and I have no other time to eat dinner.

KVR: Can you give an example of a typical dish you'll have for each meal of the day?

BM: I'll have five meals each day. For breakfast, I would do scrambled egg whites packed with every type of vegetable that you can think of: peppers, onions, mushrooms, zucchini and squash. Then I'd add some cheese, maybe a little sour cream. For my next meal, I'll have a protein shake and a piece of fruit.

For lunch, I've been having a lot of soups and salads lately. I'll go to Jason's Deli or Panera Bread and I'll do a half sandwich and salad, a half sandwich and soup, or just a soup and salad. So, for the soup, I'll have something like a butternut squash, or broccoli and cheese (of course something with no meat in it). I'll have a salad of any type. For the following meal, I'll have a protein bar with a fruit...nothing too big.

For dinner, my last meal of the day, I would do something like salmon and a salad with avocado. I love avocados. I'll even whip some guacamole up and put some guacamole on my salad. I make random things.

I've also learned to cook with the no-meat vegetarian crumbles. I do a thing called "Recipe Rehab" and I will "rehab" all of my favorite meals. My mom made casseroles and things like that when I was growing up, so now I'll substitute the meat out and I'll put the meatless crumbles in it. So, I still get to eat stuff like tacos and spaghetti...all of my favorites. Because I was a food addict, which is a real thing, I had to find ways to still be happy with what I was taking in for my body. I lived a certain way for twenty years of my life. Growing up, food was just so good...I don't know how to put it any other way. I had to figure out a way to eat and still be happy while knowing I'm making better choices for myself.

I think it's important to try different things out, because you don't really know what you will like until you try it. I've found a lot of fun things in the meatless frozen department. They get me by. I think one is called "Amy's"...she makes a bunch of meatless substitutes. They make meatless lasagna that I really like to get. So I've found different ways to eliminate any excuses not to eat right.

KVR: What are some foods that you normally avoid, but crave?

BM: I've been craving chicken wings, but I can't eat them at all. So, I had to find a way around that and I bake potatoes now. I'll do baked potatoes, roasted potatoes and then I'll put buffalo sauce on them so they can get that "wing" flavoring. Then I'll put a little blue cheese crumble on top instead of the dressing to cut the calories down.

KVR: What are some of your all-time favorite foods?

BM: Philly cheesesteak. Oh my gosh...Philly cheesesteaks are amazing. The thing is I don't eat that anymore since I don't eat meat now. So instead, I'll order the peppers, onions and mushrooms and put them in a hoagie with cheese and it's still really good.

KVR: What are some of your all-time least favorite foods?

BM: It would be anything on the more exotic side of things. I eat pretty much any fruit and vegetable you can think of down to a rutabaga, down to a leek...so I eat mostly everything that you can think of. I'm OK on snails, fish eggs and stuff like that. Now, if we're going country...soul food with chitlins, pig's feet and stuff like that—those are the types of things my parents would cook when I was growing up and I was like "Y'all gonna have to pass me up on that." Not for me.

KVR: What are some of your favorite restaurants?

BM: I love Philly cheesesteaks from Woody's in Atlanta, but without the meat. These places are all in Atlanta...I really like Doc Green's. I like Siva's. They have an amazing salmon with rice and Greek salad that I get. Oh, and their stuffed mushrooms...oh my goodness. For something more generic, I like Olive Garden. That's been a childhood favorite. I have my favorite Mexican spot called La Parrilla. I go to American Deli for my wings. I go to specific places for specific things.

KVR: When you go grocery shopping, are there any certain foods or beverages that you'll often get?

BM: Brussels sprouts. Brussels sprouts have to be in the bag. Spinach has to be in the bag. Kale. I have to get veggie crumbles for my spaghetti or tacos. I can make those quickly and eat them for three days. Definitely watermelon, pineapple, mango, strawberries, blueberries, raspberries...all the berries. Almond milk. Those are the things I'll normally put in my buggy. Honestly, I'll also get sorbet with actual fruit in it too. So when I want something sweet, I'll get that as opposed to ice cream.

KVR: One of the biggest obstacles people face with weight loss is dealing with their food cravings. How do you deal with yours?

BM: I create ways around it. Like I mentioned with the chicken wings earlier, I had to come up with something else. I have to do what works with my mentality.

For example, I worked with some obese girls here in Atlanta for an organization called Choices. We had a summer camp program going on this week where we were teaching the girls how to make healthier foods, how to make healthier choices, how to read nutrition labels. It was a lot of empowerment workshops, self-esteem and things like that. I was helping with the confidence and physical side of things. I shared that my mentality for working out and doing the things I had to do was, "I'm just gonna do it cause I know I can." I've done so much at this point with my body with what I'm eating and with my workouts. Earlier today, I just hopped on my bike from my house and rode to camp. Then I rode about six-and-a-half miles to South Cobb. It took me forty minutes, but I did it.

When people think so little of themselves and their abilities, they limit themselves. I operate on a "no limit" mentality. Of course I have my days when I'm on the struggle bus and I'm like "Yeah, I don't even feel like doing it today." But, I always tap back in the next day because I can't let it go on too long.

The show I did, Extreme Weight Loss, gave us so many great tools to stay committed to it. It's just up to you. I know I've done so much and once your mind is stretched, it can never go back. I know what I'm capable of. If I say I'm going to hop on my bike and take a bike ride today, that's the intention that I set and I have to complete that intention. If I don't, then it adds back into the guilty mindset and feeling like you can't accomplish it. It feeds into the negative side of the brain.

FITNESS

KVR: How would you describe your natural body type? Lean, athletic, curvy, or a combination?

BM: I'm definitely more curvy. The smallest I've gotten down to was 190 pounds and my BMI is high as well. At my smallest, I think I looked too skinny so I had to beef myself back up a little bit. I love being an advocate for the plus-size community. I have a shirt I have that says "I've never been a size 2." And truthfully, I never really wanted to be. I always wanted to be the healthiest version of myself. I'm happy in my size 12 and 14s. I'm happy at 230. Of course, I'm still looking at getting skin removal surgery which will make things make sense a little more. Without that, I look a lot bigger than I actually am. A lot of times, people will pre-judge my abilities or the type of lifestyle that I actually live just because they see what I look like.

KVR: How much did you weigh at your heaviest and how much have you actually lost since then?

BM: I weighed 400 pounds at my heaviest and I have taken off over 180 pounds.

KVR: What do you tell people who have given up on exercise or eating right because they think their metabolism or genetics are against them?

BM: I tell people to stop focusing on the scale. Stop focusing on the scale, because when you are bound to that scale, it can dictate your joy, it can dictate these victories...and there are so many "non-scale" victories that you can enjoy. I feel like if people focus on their eating, if they focus on their exercise, the weight will come off. Even if it doesn't come off as quickly as they want it to, the most important thing is for people to realize that they are making healthier choices. Just within that, they are serving themselves justice.

A lot of people ask me why I haven't had skin removal surgery. I tell them, well there are still a lot of people who need to see this body. They need to see that you can love yourself regardless of what you've got going on. What matters is your commitment to yourself, your personal integrity. Keeping those promises is a great feeling.

KVR: Scientific studies have shown that very fit people can come in different shapes and sizes. Sadly, when people think of the word "fit," they only have one body type in mind. What have you done or what are you doing to help dispel this myth?

BM: I'm living my life out loud, sharing my experiences and what I'm doing with people. I'm asking them to come with me and be a "Brandi bestie." If you want to sign up for a 5K, I'll do a 5K with you. If I am signed up to do a 5K, I'm opening it up to everybody and I'm inviting people saying, "Hey, this is a judgment-free zone." The majority of everything I do is for the plus-size community. We did a 5K called the "Plus Strut" for women sized 12 and up. I wish there were things like that when I was growing up. So, I try to "be that change" so to speak. To show people that I can love myself at this size, I just exude it. To show people that I can work out at this size and kill it, I just do it. People gonna talk. You just gotta give them new stuff to talk about. They can make assumptions before they know me, but I love proving people wrong.

KVR: Do you have any other go-to exercises of physical activities?

BM: I do dance fitness, biking, hiking, swimming, CrossFit, 5Ks...I've done a half Iron Man before. I love MMA fighting, so I've done some of that. They had us doing a bunch of different things and I found so many things that I really like to do from that.

KVR: One of your dancing videos actually became a viral sensation. Why do you think that resonated with so many people?

BM: I think people are tired of being judged and I'm a breath of fresh air when it comes to confidently not making any excuses and just loving yourself. People saw me dancing free with what they like to call "the jiggle" and not really caring what anybody would think about it. I think it speaks volumes to people who live their lives "boxed in."

I feel like if others see me living freely, they say "If Brandi can do it, I can do it too." I've gotten messages from people saying, "Ever since I've been following you, I've lost 30 pounds." Also, "when you post something and it pushes me forward." It's words like *that* that lets me know that I need to keep sharing this stuff cause it's working.

KVR: At what point would you say you felt happy and confident with your overall fitness?

BM: I would say probably for the past year since I found dance and became an instructor. That's when. However, there were activities that I always liked and made me feel good. I like to run. I like to bike. Swim. Those were things that were always really enjoyable for me.

KVR: What keeps you motivated to maintain such a high level of fitness and activity?

BM: Honestly, not wanting to put the weight back on and not ever wanting to backslide. I promised myself I would never forget how far I've come and how I never want to feel like I did at my heaviest ever again. I was always pretty happy and outgoing, but my energy level wasn't the same...I can't quite explain it, but there was a huge difference. I remember thinking, "I need to find a chair and sit down" even when I was just standing in one spot. Now, I want to be up and moving around. I want to be in the action and enjoy life.

KVR: What has been the hardest part of your weight loss journey and how have you overcome that?

BM: The hardest part of my weight loss journey would have to be looking in the mirror, knowing that it looks different, but not seeing the full picture. Sometimes that can be defeating. I can see little ab indentations and stuff like that, but I have body dysmorphia so when I look in the mirror, I don't see what other people see, unless they show me pictures of myself to compare. To me, when I look in the mirror, I feel like I look just as big as the day I started losing weight. That's still something I have to work through personally...and it just takes time. So when I'm looking in the mirror and feeling down on myself, I'll just take a picture and compare it to a previous picture of myself and think, "Okay, I'm good. I'm still good."

KVR: Any other tips of advice regarding health, fitness or eating?

BM: You can fall without failing as long as you confess, reassess and recommit. That's literally all you have to do. That's one of the biggest tools that I got from Extreme Weight Loss.

If you sit down for three months and decide, "You know what, I'm tired, I don't have time" or any other excuse in the book and put on 25 or 30 pounds within that time period, the only thing that would cause you to fail is deciding not to start over...deciding not to do it again. I think of women who have kids. I know a lot of women who have lost weight, then became pregnant and put the weight back on. If you put weight back on, all you have to do is think that every day is a new day to start over. As long as you have life and breath in your body, you can literally recommit to yourself and continue your journey. It's a lifestyle change, a lifetime commitment. You can pick up where you left off...and that's all it is.

Nick Santonastasso

"THE BIGGEST DISABILITY IS A BAD MINDSET."

NICK SANTONASTASSO

Nick Santonastasso is an internationally-known bodybuilder, fitness model and motivational speaker. What sets Nick apart from others in his field (and in life) is that he was born with Hanhart syndrome, a rare birth defect that left him without legs, an underdeveloped right arm and a left arm with one finger. However, his absence of limbs is overcome by his abundance of will and determination.

FOOD

- Type of eater: Omnivore—Yeah, I eat anything. I'm Italian, so definitely an omnivore.

- Adventurous level: 8—I don't think I'm a full 10, but I'm pretty adventurous. One of the things I like to do when we travel is to experience the culture through the food.
- Taste preferences: sweet, salty, spicy
- Ethnicity: I'm Italian and Portuguese. My dad's side is mostly Italian and my mom is Portuguese. I need to do an ancestry test, but as far as I know, I'm Italian and Portuguese.

KVR: Do you attribute any of your tastes to your ethnicity is there something else in particular that you give credit to for your taste preferences?

NS: I think in some ways I'm a bad Italian. What I mean by that is that I still don't like wine. I'm still trying to acquire a taste for wine and a love for wine. Just like oil and vinegar for salads or dipping the bread...I don't really do that. I think I'm just very open with my tastes and always try to get out of my comfort zone and eat food that's not just Italian. I like to try everyone's food.

KVR: What are your favorite cuisines?

NS: I like Mexican food. I like Italian food. I like Thai food. I like Chinese food. I also like the [Japanese] hibachi style of eating. I don't like sushi, which is really weird cause all bodybuilders love sushi. It looks great, but I don't like it. I mean it looks amazing and I wish I liked it, but I don't. I think I'm just a very open person and I can find a love in all foods. But I think my main ones, like I said are Italian, Mexican and Spanish, Thai...and Korean BBQ as well. I'm a foodie for sure.

KVR: Do you follow a certain diet being a bodybuilder? Do you follow a meal plan? How does it work for you?

NS: I still have the same coach that put me through my first prep. I think it's super important even if you're in off-season or even if you're balancing your life to always have a coach to send your check-ins to and hold you accountable. If you don't have a coach, you're more inclined to not do anything and I know I'd be that guy. Right now, I am on a certain amount of macros and one of my biggest struggles is trying to balance the travel...I'm traveling all over and staying on point with macros. I'm at this very different part of my life where I'm learning balance.

KVR: Can you give me an example of a typical dish for each meal of the day?

NS: Yeah, so right now I'm eating like a dog and it's really plain stuff cause I really want to dial in. So a typical meal for me right now would be 6 ounces of protein like ground beef or turkey and 1 cup of jasmine rice...that would be one meal. I don't think that's much food, to be honest. My coach called me out on undereating, so I think I might have to up my eating.

I love rice. Rice is my go-to. Jasmine rice is amazing. When you really dial yourself in and you don't eat sugary stuff, you start craving weird things. I was craving cream of rice...It's kind of like oatmeal, but it's like instant rice. I craved almond butter and rice cakes in my prep—that was like your sweets or your dessert. I remember having a protein shake and being able to use almond milk and thinking that was the best thing on the planet when I was in prep. It's cool to figure out healthy alternatives that still taste really good. Like almond milk is a game-changer.

It was definitely a struggle growing up in my family. Dinner was like three carbs and one protein. We also drank the red cap milk, like the fattiest milk, which I love...so my parents did it do me. I grew up in Bayville, NJ which is basically the Jersey shore until I was 18 and came down to Florida for fitness.

KVR: What are some of the foods that you would normally avoid, but crave?

NS: Pasta. Eating a meal that doesn't have any protein in it, so it's all carbs. It's super hard to do that now, but I love penne and vodka, mac 'n cheese, the really bad foods that have no nutritional value. Those are probably the main things I crave. Also, one of my weak-spots is Cold Stone. I love ice cream.

KVR: What are some of your all-time favorite foods? If you were to have a last meal, what would you include?

NS: It would definitely include Cold Stone. Ice cream would definitely be there. Penne and vodka would definitely be there. My dad makes great raviolis with a clear garlic sauce. Mac and cheese for sure. I like burgers too. Sweet potato fries are one of my faves. Yeah, it's more of the carbs right? Also all different types of pastas. That's my weakness. Oh, and tacos...don't forget tacos. I like spicy chicken or chicken verde with pico on it and cheese. My go-to's are chicken and steak tacos.

KVR: What are some of your all-time least favorite foods?

NS: I hate pickles. That's another food that looks good, but I don't like it. I'm sick of broccoli from prep, so I don't eat broccoli anymore. I'm sick of asparagus unless it's grilled. I'm not a fan of Brussels sprouts. My go-to vegetable is green beans. I could eat green beans all day every day. I don't like tofu. I'm not a fan of spinach. I pretty much just try to find the vegetables that I like and stick with them only because I don't like many.

KVR: What are your favorite restaurants around where you live or anywhere you visited?

NS: We just got back from Hawaii and there were food trucks. We were looking for authentic Hawaiian food. So there were food trucks and they made this...I don't know what it's called, but it's spicy chicken with rice...and that's all I need, chicken and rice. There's also this place that made fresh ice smoothies. I'm a big fan of watermelon, so we had these watermelon smoothies.

Here in Tampa, there's a place called Miguelito's and they make amazing tacos, especially on Taco Tuesdays. We have a steakhouse in Tampa called Berns. It's the #1 steakhouse in America. It's super amazing. If Cold Stone counts as a restaurant, I love their ice cream. I can get really bad...my favorite fast food is Whoppers from Burger King. I love Burger King, which is really bad. Oh, and I gotta add In-N-Out. Whenever I'm over there [on the west coast], I gotta get In-N-Out.

Other than that, I find hole-in-the-wall Italian restaurants that are hidden gems. It's kinda hard to find some good pizza and bagels out here. I'm from Jersey and New York, so gotta go up there for that. Other than that I don't have any other restaurants that really stick out.

KVR: What are some of your favorite food and beverage products?

NS: I don't drink it remotely as much as I did as a kid, but I love chocolate milk. I used to drink chocolate milk as a kid every night...that's probably why I was chubby.

Food, for me, comes down to simplicity and being able to be independent. I'm an athlete for Icon, so they basically do all my food. I like to keep it super basic. Like I said...ground turkey, ground beef, steak and I usually like to season it with sea salt, pepper and hot sauces.

I drank a lot of soda as a kid, so the one thing that helps me get over those cravings is getting those sparkling waters that taste like soda, but they're really not. Those are a game-changer, especially if you just need to trick your body into thinking you're getting a cheat...like sipping on black cherry water that tastes like Dr. Pepper. Those are my little tricks. Rather than drinking a diet soda, drink sparkling water.

I'm a fan of eggs too. I could eat eggs for any meal. I just try to keep it simple, to be honest. I like pancakes, but they're not as healthy. I also like acai bowls...I'm a fan for sure.

KVR: Obviously, without full limbs, your body isn't the same as the average person's body. Do you actually have to eat less than the average person?

NS: So something I realized and was telling my coach was, "Wow listen, I have the same stomach as you do. I could probably eat more."

But because of my height, I do have to eat less. It takes less to fill me out. My macros are less than other people because the protein and carbs don't have legs and full arms to go into. My macros are around 150g of protein, 50g of carbohydrates and 18g of fat. So yeah, I have to eat less than regular people.

FITNESS

KVR: How would you describe your natural body type...lean, athletic, stocky, etc.?

NS: I'm naturally fat. Before any of the sports I played, I was naturally a chubby kid. My dad was a big dude, very strong, but not lean. My mom is super skinny. I have 2 sisters and 1 brother and they're all older. My oldest sister was a gymnast, so she was an athlete. My brother was a wrestler and my other sister was a tennis and softball player. She used to tease me for having a gut...she had a six-pack. I don't think I was active enough and definitely not lean. Now I'm in the best shape out of everyone in my family, which is wild.

I'm still learning my genetics, so I'm still building this person. I'm one of those people whose hard work triumphs genetics. I just work my ass off in the gym. When I'm training it's balls to the wall. When I was on that prep, I was like "all or nothing"...that's why I got the results I got.

191

I was just a chubby kid. To give you an example, for wrestling...to wrestle varsity you had to weigh at least 85 pounds to wrestle 106. So, I was stuffing my face to gain weight. I was the chubby wrestler doing the opposite of everyone else. In high school, I was 85 pounds and chunky. Then throughout my fitness training, when I step on stage I was 77 pounds shredded. Now, I'm sitting at 95 pounds with abs. I'm still growing, I'm in my bulk right now and I'm 22, so I know my body's very receptive. I'm still trying to learn more about my body and it's an ongoing process. I don't think I naturally had muscle, so I definitely built this person.

KVR: Do you have any go-to exercises or physical activities that you do?

NS: Yeah, a lot of my work is resistance work, or band work. One of the things that helps me is band work and telling whoever is working with me to match the weight on my left side to my right side...making things symmetrical and pushing the same amount of weight on both sides. A lot of my chest work is with resistance bands. I'm doing band presses and having my buddies push on me on different angles. My back is probably the most impressive part of me with how wide it is. A lot of my training, to be honest, is just band work, resistance work and hooking up the cables.

I'm figuring out what's most efficient and what tears through the muscle the most and gets the biggest pump. I think that's a big thing for people...not going to the gym and ego lifting, but using weight where you can really work through the muscle and control it on both movements.

When I first started lifting, my form was shit. I didn't even know what I was doing. Going through my prep, my buddy Cody (who trains me now) was like a "form Nazi." Now, I'm really strict on my form and on point with everything.

KVR: At what point in your life were you actually happy with your overall fitness?

NS: When I started my fitness journey, I remember saying to myself, "Ok. I'm gonna walk on the treadmill for 30 minutes and in 3-6 months I'll have a shredded six-pack." So, that's how I started my fitness journey and then I realized, "Oh shit, there's much more to this."

The thing with me is that my right side of my body is underdeveloped. When you guys are born with legs and walking around, you're automatically building up your obliques, you're already building up your lower back and you're already building up your abs cause that's what you use when you walk. With me walking a bit differently, my left side is a little bit more defined. I'm still working on my last two abs. They're still not here...We'll, they're almost here, but they're not here.

There was a time when I would take a picture early in my career and I'm like "Oh my God, I'm making progress." But then, you know how it is...on to the next. It's like, "I need to get better." Even when I committed to my bodybuilding show, I knew that my symmetry wasn't gonna be where it needed to be. I knew that my right side wasn't gonna be fully developed and I wasn't gonna have all my abs. When I was super shredded for my show, I was still looking at myself like, "Fuck, your right side isn't where you want it to be." I'm really hard on myself, to be honest. But, I was super proud of myself for my "ride-or-die" mentality with that prep. I never skipped a diet, never skipped a workout and so I was super proud of that for sure.

KVR: During your fitness journey, how long did it take for you to achieve that point where you were happy with where you were at?

NS: It's been 3 years. I could probably say that third year (when I was in my prep), that was when I was happiest. So it took me 3 years of figuring out how to become the best. I realized I fell in love with the wrong sport, because bodybuilding is the most time-consuming sport of fitness in itself. It just doesn't happen overnight. You know, we're primed; we want everything instantly. We can go on our phones and Facetime people and watch movies instantly. Then you look at fitness and you gotta work years and sculpt your body...and don't slip up for a month cause then it looks like you didn't do anything.

KVR: What keeps you motivated to maintain such a high level of fitness?

NS: One part of my motivation is that it's my base. I built most of my following around fitness. If I fell off and went and got fat, people would be like, "Dude, what are you doing?" Also, it comes back to perspective. I know there are millions of kids and adults who are confined in wheelchairs and confined in hospital beds who would do anything and everything just to go outside for a day. So when you look at it like that, if I'm given the opportunity to be able to get to the gym and back to my house independently and go through a workout and get my body into shape, I'm gonna do it because there's people out there that can't. So, now it's a staple. I'm stuck with it.

KVR: Anything else you want to add? Any tips or advice regarding health, fitness or eating?

NS: Yeah, just for people to realize that it's not a sprint or a race. Changing little habits here and there, like little steps at a time are gonna become one big step. You'll be like "Oh my God, I'm seeing progress." It's just the little things.

Even when I fell off, I noticed the importance of getting my water in daily. Having your body know it's getting a gallon of water a day, you'll naturally speed up your metabolism. Your body will naturally hold less water weight because it knows it's getting this water every day. Not only does it help with your skin and everything, but there's just little things, little tweaks in your life that will be a game-changer for you.

If people are starting off and they've never started eating clean...you don't even need to start eating clean at first. Just start eating smaller portions so you speed up your metabolism. That's a little hack. If you don't want to change up what you're eating, just make it smaller portions and eat like 5 to 6 portions a day. Rather than eating two massive meals and slowing your metabolism down.

Now, I'm contradicting myself cause I have a coach, but look at Arnold [Schwarzenegger]. Arnold didn't have a coach. Those guys didn't have coaches back then. They learned through trial and error. Just take a sense of comfort in that it's your journey and that things that work for other people aren't necessarily gonna work for you. The carbs that work for other people might not work for you. Everything's split testing. Even now, to this day, I'm still figuring out what carbs work most efficiently for me and what carbs bloat me. It's all trial and error. Just get excited at the fact that you get to try and test new things. There's not one golden road that's gonna get everyone there; there's multiple paths. Find your own lane. Find what works for you.

To wrap it all up...I love tacos.

Nikki Sharp

Nikki Sharp is a health and fitness expert, author and international model. Her mission is "to spread the knowledge of healthy living for the mind, body and soul."

FOOD

- Type of eater: Omnivore, but primarily plant-based—I call myself "a vegan who cheats." My biggest thing is that for ethical, environmental and health reasons, we should absolutely be eating way less animal products. At the same time, I don't believe it's my job to judge anybody else. It's my

198

job to inform people that certain things are healthier than others.

- Adventurous level: 5—I'm willing to try just about anything, but with that I don't eat any fish. If it's vegetarian-based I'm ok to try anything. I'm very adventurous for my own personal lifestyle, but I wouldn't go to a restaurant and just order whatever's available.

- Taste preferences: salty & bitter—Because I drink red wine, I find that I have less cravings for anything sugary. The only time I really crave sugar is if I haven't slept enough and I'm tired. Otherwise, my body just really likes salt. I try to eat as much home-cooked food as I can and because of that, I don't monitor how much salt I eat.

- Ethnicity: I am Swiss-English. Both of my parents are British and my grandmother was Swiss. I have a lot of Swiss genes from her. I was born in the US, but the rest of my family outside of my mother and father live in the UK.

KVR: Do you attribute any of your taste preferences to your ethnicity, or is there something else that you give credit to for your tastes?

NS: No, I didn't really eat any British food as I was born in America. My mother cooked a homemade dinner for me every night and I ate a lot of fresh meals, but at the same time I did grow up having Lunchables and other things from the standard American diet, like pizza and tacos for school lunches.

Now that I'm older, I definitely identify with the European culture far more than I do American because of the higher quality of food. You can eat all the things the "bad things" that are attributed as "bad" in America like cheese and bread and things that would cause you to break out, feel bloated or get constipated. In Europe, you eat small quantities of food but it's all about quality over quantity.

The American way and the culture that we have, sadly, has been about excess and quick fixes. People aren't willing to put in the work for things, but then they stuff themselves and try to starve themselves afterwards.

I give credit to my mother because she taught me about cooking fresh food. She taught me to go to the farmer's market and how to smell fruits and vegetables. I was never into food growing up, but as I got older, I started having an appreciation because she would make homemade pasta for me and really got me understanding how to appreciate different tastes. So she's very much the person I would model my current food habits after.

KVR: What are some of your favorite cuisines?

NS: Definitely Italian. Anything with pasta and cheese...and pizza and wine. I love Japanese food even though I don't eat fish because they have a lot of vegetables. Their cuisine is very veggie heavy. I just find it very clean. I love the different herbs and spices they use in Mexican food, like cilantro and chili peppers. I'd say those are my biggest. So yeah, I love French, Italian and Japanese style cuisine. I feel like every American as well is like "Pasta, pizza, bread, wine? Yes, please."

KVR: Do you follow a certain diet or meal plan, or pretty much eat what you want?

NS: I eat what I want when I want. I don't diet. This is coming after years of dieting and eating disorders. I very much focus on just eating real food grown in the earth or made by hand. For example, cheese in France is made by hand, but cheese in America is usually made in a factory so I avoid it at all costs. I don't eat veal, chicken or turkey. I do eat a really good quality piece of meat once in a while. Other than that, I'm much more vegetarian. I just feel best that way.

KVR: What initially led you to become more vegetarian and lean towards plant-based meals?

NS: It's interesting because there's nothing really that necessarily led me there. The more I listened to my body and the more intuitively I ate, the better I felt. It was a very natural evolution.

When I was younger I tried to be fully vegan and raw vegan. I tried all the different diets. Anytime you do a diet that is restrictive, it doesn't work. I kept failing and feeling guilty. Finally, I just started focusing on the foods that made me feel best and the most energetic. I would wake up and crave those foods and not feel guilty afterwards. That's how I started leaning towards more of a plant-based diet.

I never once told myself you can't have something. It was more of, "Will this make me feel good after I eat it?" I've learned now that I can go to the farmer's market and get some incredibly good quality cheese and buy just enough to eat for that moment so I'm satisfied. It surprises people, but I eat bread whenever I want. I eat pasta when I want, but I'm very mindful about portion sizes and the energy that goes into it. I would say I've been primarily eating plant-based foods for about five years now. It's an evolution every day.

I coach people on this all the time: The more you focus on what you can't have, or don't allow yourself the things that bring you joy, the more you're going to binge on them. It's about the way you eat the foods you want. You do end up losing weight and getting the body you want while enjoying the foods you really like, but you have to eat in very mindful ways that bring you more joy.

KVR: Can you give me examples of typical dishes you'll have for breakfast, lunch and dinner?

NS: Yeah, for breakfast I'll always have a coffee or a matcha latte with almond milk. I love having avocado toast, so I'll mash up an avocado and put it on Ezekiel bread, but in Europe I'll have any kind of bread. Sometimes I'll put a fried egg on it.

For lunch, I'll have a salad, which is always predominantly raw, but I love putting lots of things to add to the texture. So, I'll include things like: cucumber, carrots, avocados, black beans, quinoa, edamame and homemade hummus. I like my salads to be really big and a full bowl of nourishment.

Then for dinner, I'll have something cooked that's a little more hearty like a soup. In general, I find that when I snack it's just nuts or a banana. I'm not a huge snacker. I prefer to eat three meals, but all are quite big and full of carbs, protein and fats. It ranges, but that's kind of it for the most part.

KVR: What are some foods you would normally avoid, but crave like "cheat day" foods?

NS: First of all, I hate calling it "cheat day." That's just my thing. I feel like that vilifies food and it says that what you're eating is bad.

Outside of that, I really love pizza. Every once in a while, I give myself permission to have a Domino's pizza...like the shittiest of the bad pizzas for you, but it's a very conscious decision. I know that I haven't had it in a very long time and I don't feel guilty cause I'll split it with a friend or I'll go to a really nice pizza shop and get some good quality slices.

I don't order pasta all the time, but when I do, I always choose to get it from restaurants where I know it's going to be really delicious and worth every bite.

Also, desserts. In Paris, pastries and croissants are everywhere, but I don't have a lot of them because I don't crave sweets as much. But if I'm with a friend and we want to share a pastry, it's not an issue. So yeah, those are my big three.

KVR: What are some of your all-time favorite foods? If you were to have a last meal, what would you include?

NS: Well, "last meal" is different from "all-time favorite" because, for the last meal, you can go as crazy as you want. My daily food that I'm obsessed with is hummus. Hummus is my go-to everything. I like every type of hummus available. It's so strange, but I really *really* love Thai sweet potato soup. I have a recipe in my book "Meal Prep Your Way to Weight Loss" and I'm obsessed with it. It's something I go to quite often. I really love cucumber salads and seaweed salads at Japanese restaurants. Those are my favorite. I'm also obsessed with avocado toast. Those are foods that I tend to eat quite often.

Then for my last meal, it's all my "cheat stuff": pizza, something with barbecue sauce...that sort of thing. (Although we don't call it cheat meals!)

KVR: What are some of your all-time least favorite foods?

NS: Very strangely, I don't like raw tomatoes. I love cooked tomatoes if they're blended into a sauce. I just cannot handle the taste of raw tomato. I gag from it, so I always remove those. I don't do raw onions. Those are definitely my two biggest ones. Also, if anything comes with foie gras or caviar, that's a no-go. But in terms of everyday American-style foods, I'd say raw onions and raw tomatoes. Well, and pork belly or various meats (pretty much anything other than filet mignon) gross me out.

KVR: What are some of your favorite restaurants and why?

NS: One of my top favorites is called Plant Food and Wine in LA. It's by a friend of mine. It's a vegan restaurant, but the food is impeccable. I love taking people there who are not vegan because a lot of the stuff there, you'd just have no idea that it's vegan. That and Crossroads (also in LA) are both vegan and they're just incredible. At Crossroads, you can get things and think "There's literally no way this is vegan, zero chance." They do a carbonara with an egg, but it's all vegan and you're just like, "Wow." I love Sunset Tower in LA as well. It's just a very chic, elegant old school restaurant in LA.

I would also say Lulu's in Paris. It has a view of the Eiffel Tower and is over by the Louvre museum. It has great food and a great atmosphere. It's one of those restaurants that just nailed it.

KVR: When you go grocery shopping, do you have any favorite foods or beverages that you usually get?

NS: Let's see. I get soda water...I get La Croix. That's about it. I don't drink a lot of stuff other than water, sparkling water and wine. I personally love water, so I don't need anything else. I'll sometimes put tea in a big bottle or jug of water and drink that.

In terms of food, I always get broccoli to steam. I always get avocados and cucumbers. I love having kimchi in my fridge. I always get an organic hummus if I'm not able to make it. I always have a bottle of red wine in my pantry as I'm living in Paris, and, well, that's what you do as a Parisian. And you can always find a can or two of chickpeas, black beans or kidney beans.

FITNESS

KVR: How would you describe your natural body type? Are you naturally lean, athletic or curvy?

NS: I'm naturally lean. But if I start to eat outside of what I'm doing right now, although I won't gain weight easily, I can get skinny fat quite easily, meaning I gain weight on my hips, thighs and stomach and get cellulite. I have a long lean build. I'm very lucky for that, but I work very hard to maintain a good body as well.

KVR: Do you have any go-to exercises or physical activities?

NS: I love doing high-intensity training outside or on the treadmill. I do five minutes of warm-up, then twenty seconds of sprinting and ten seconds of jumping side-to-side. I love lifting weights and I love yoga. So, for me, that's kind of all I really do. I really love walking everywhere I can. I love hiking. On a day-to-day basis, it's doing high-intensity interval training, it's doing circuit training by incorporating burpees or jump squats and things that elevate your heart rate as well as tone your body...plus yoga.

KVR: At what point in your life were you happy with your overall fitness?

NS: Right now. I feel best about my body because I eat what I want. I'm not obsessive. I don't deprive myself. I exercise because I love to feel good, not because I'm trying to punish myself for eating something. I honestly feel better than I ever have in my life.

KVR: How long did it take for you to reach that point?

NS: It's been a few years to really get to a very intuitive place with myself. I would say over the past year, I've really paid attention to foods that make me feel good and how I wanted to wake up and feel throughout the day. That's when it became a lot easier.

KVR: What actually keeps you motivated to maintain such a high level of fitness?

NS: I actually do less fitness now than I ever have. That's a little bit interesting for me. For example, I didn't go to the gym the other day, but I walked 5 kilometers around the city. Fitness and exercise is no longer "Oh I need to go to the gym today." I've actually worked out less and have seen more results. The key is...if you go to the gym and don't like it, you're never gonna see the results you want because you're basically reinforcing a negative belief that you don't like it. But, when you change it so you're doing something you love...say you love walking, if you dedicate thirty minutes to walking five days a week because you love how it makes you feel, you'll see results far quicker. So yes, everyone needs to move their body, but whatever makes you feel good...that is 100% what you should do and nothing else. Don't pay attention to people who say "go do CrossFit" or "go to SoulCycle," because if you dread going or don't want to do it, then you're continuing a negative thought pattern and a negative cycle of something that will not positively affect you long term.

KVR: Any additional tips in regards to fitness or eating?

NS: You have to stop looking at food like an enemy like it's going to make you fat or that you have to cut something out to lose weight. When you start to change your perception on what things make you feel good and how you want to feel energetically—like "Do you want to feel light? Do you want to feel happy?"—*then* it becomes easier to continue to make the right choices. It's all about shifting your mind from a negative perception about food and exercise to one of being positive. For myself, if I would binge on food or eat too much, I would not allow myself to go to the gym the next day because I didn't want my mind to think "Oh you're just going to the gym because you messed up." I wanted to go to the gym when I felt great and therefore, I started going to the gym more and more and loving it and seeing bigger results. I'm very passionate about that right now. It's all about changing your perception on what you do and what you eat.

Kelli Tennant

Kelli Tennant is the host of Ceremony Wellness, a podcast centered on how to "integrate modern healing with ancient wisdom." She has battled with chronic illness for over a decade and has made it her life's mission to help others on their healing journeys.

FOOD

- Type of eater: Carnivore—I follow the paleo lifestyle.
- Adventurous level: 7 or 8—I don't really say "no" to a lot of foods.
- Taste preferences: savory

- Ethnicity: I am half Mexican and half Swedish.

KVR: Do you attribute any of your tastes to your ethnicity?

KT: Yes, and if I say "no" my mother will kill me, haha. My mom is the Mexican one and she's the most incredible cook, so I grew up eating really *really* good well-made food.

KVR: What are some of your favorite cuisines?

KT: I love Mexican. I love Italian. Those are probably my favorite.

KVR: You mentioned following the paleo diet. How exactly did you get into it and how long have you been doing it for?

KT: I've had chronic illness for about 14 years and was very very sick. I was on a lot of medication. Because of that, I was trying to figure out ways on how to holistically heal, so I found this concept of using food as medicine and that led me to the paleo diet which I started in 2012. I've basically been on different variations of the paleo diet since then. I've done a specific autoimmune protocol that falls under that. It was really about eliminating inflammatory foods and triggers that contributed to my autoimmune disease and inflammation as well as really understanding that there are so many foods out there that are healing, really nourishing and delicious that can alter the state of your body and the way that you feel. That impacts hormone function, your gut and your brain.

So, for me, it was really about healing and also understanding food in a different way. Instead of just putting stuff in your mouth to eat, it was about, "How can I use this to heal?" At the same time, I wanted to make sure I was feeling satisfied and not restricting myself or missing out on delicious things.

KVR: How did you originally find discover this way of eating?

KT: I think my boyfriend at the time was really into food and keto, things like that. He's the one that brought it up to and I found this whole community that was using food as medicine through paleo specifically.

KVR: Can you give me examples of typical dishes you'll have throughout the day? Any go-to snacks?

KT: Yeah, right now I just made what's called a "pagel." It's made with cassava and almond flour with sunflower seed butter on it. So, that's something I'll normally have. I do smoked salmon, scrambled eggs and greens in the morning quite a bit.

I do a lot of mixed greens with olive oil and lemon with either chicken or baked salmon or burgers. I'll just rotate the kind of meat that I'm having. I like to do organ meat. So I'll get ground heart, liver and beef at the butcher shop and make burgers or chili with that. It's really good. It's super nourishing and really dense.

I also make a ton of foods with a ton of vegetables, so I'll just roast a giant pan of veggies with bone broth or pureed cauliflower. That will be a vegetarian paleo option for me.

I'm not really a big snacker, but I'll do Jilz Crackers sometimes which is a paleo cracker with flax seeds. I'll have that with vegan cashew cheese. Other than that, maybe some nuts, but I don't really snack.

KVR: What are some foods that you would normally avoid, but crave? Any "cheat day" foods?

KT: I don't eat a lot of rice, but that's definitely one of my first go-to's when I want to cheat. That's why the whole sushi conversation is awesome.

I love pizza...and you can make a paleo pizza, but I'll use a gluten-free crust since I can't have gluten. I'm allergic. So, I'll do a gluten-free pizza at some of my favorite pizza places...or pancakes, waffles...carbs basically.

KVR: What are some of your all-time favorite foods?

KT: This isn't paleo, but I always say that if I was going to die tomorrow, I would want my mom's chicken tacos and chile relleno. I grew up on that. She makes them amazing. They're these fried tortilla shells, chicken, homemade guacamole and salsa. Then her chile rellenos...I love spicy food with cheese, so I love her chile rellenos which are fried and battered. So yeah, that's pretty delicious.

KVR: What are some of your all-time least favorite foods?

KT: Being Mexican, cow tongue is a big thing in our culture and my mom has made it, but it just sounds so horrific to me. Just the idea of what the texture is like with the taste buds...I don't know. I don't want anything to do with that.

KVR: What are some of your favorite restaurants and why?

KT: I love this place called True Food Kitchen. Everything is farm-to-table, organic, grass-fed, wild-caught, etc. They have a lot of vegan options. I've tried to stay away from dairy, so that always makes things easy for dessert. Their food is also really high quality, so I love it.

Same kind of concept, Granville, which is in West Hollywood is farm-to-table, no vegetable oils, really clean, a lot of paleo options. My favorite pizza place here is Pizzana in Brentwood. They have a gluten-free crust and it's to-die-for. I also love Sugarfish sushi here.

My absolute favorite restaurant though is Uchi is in Austin. It's a sushi place…So good. They have one in Denver too and I'm dying to go there.

KVR: When you go grocery shopping, do you have any favorite food or beverage items you'll usually get?

KT: Yes, my boyfriend and I love Boochcraft Kombucha. Love Bija Bhar…They call it a "resilience turmeric elixir" and it's really yummy to mix in hot water like a tea. Olipop is a really clean soda that tastes good. We love Topo Chico sparkling water. Elemental bars, which are nut and seed bars, and the Perfect Bar are great too. We also love Jillz crackers. The rest is all produce and farmer's market stuff.

FITNESS

KVR: What is your natural body type? Are you more lean, athletic, curvy, or a combination of those types?

KT: I'm definitely a combo of those things. I have big hips, but I'm more muscular and lean. I'm 6'1," so I'm definitely on the leaner side.

KVR: Do you have any go-to exercises or physical activities?

KT: I love Barry's Bootcamp. It's high-intensity interval training (HIIT). You do the treadmill, then you switch and you're on the floor doing weights and core exercises. I just really like group classes. I think they're fun.

I really like Pilates. There's a place here called Lagree and their reformer (a Pilates exercise machine) actually moves, so it lifts up and it can go side-to-side. So if you're doing a lunge on a reformer and it's moving side-to-side, you have to stay stable on that. It's really really hard and your body shakes a lot, but it's a really cool workout.

My boyfriend and I actually started boxing again and I really love that. It's such an amazing full-body workout and you get really sore. We work out at Deuce Gym as well. It's like a CrossFit-esque gym, but it's kinda just outside and you're doing heavy lifting and doing different things. It's not as crazy as CrossFit. I love that because I'm able to lift similar to the way I did in college and, for me, I get really competitive doing that and I really enjoy picking up heavy weights and doing that.

KVR: At what point would you say you were happy with your overall fitness?

KT: Well, I was really sick for 13-14 years and was bed-ridden for a lot of that. I couldn't move. Walking was too exhausting for me.

So right before I got sick, I was in incredible shape and it was the best shape I have ever been in. I was 19. Then, the next day I couldn't walk or stand up straight. I spent this whole time trying to get my body back to a place where it was strong enough to be able to handle this kind of workload and feel strong while not easily getting exhausted and feeling awful.

To be honest, this year I realized that my whole body has changed and I'm finally at a place where I'm super stoked with my fitness and what I'm able to handle and just my strength overall. It's been an interesting ride. You have a greater appreciation for the ability to move that way you want and realizing, "Wow, my body has been through all of this *and* it can still withstand it and now I'm on the other side." It's cool.

KVR: What kind of illness did you have exactly?

KT: I had Epstein-Barr virus and chronic fatigue syndrome as well as leaky gut. All of it was kind of stemming from my gut issues and microbiome. I had mono for 8 months during my freshman year at USC. Mono and Epstein-Barr come together...It's the virus that you get with mono. Actually, 90% of people have Epstein-Barr, but it may not necessarily be active in the body and mine was extremely active, really high off the charts, but no one ever tested me or treated me for it until 13 years in. That's why it was so bad, because my body was freaking out and revolting against me. I wasn't getting to the root of the problem.

Once I figured out what I actually had, did the proper treatments, took care of my body and focused on my food and healing, then I was able to get rid of it. Now I don't have any issues anymore.

KVR: What keeps you motivated to maintain such a high level of fitness at this point?

KT: It's sort of my meditation. When I don't work out, I get kind of crazy. I feel like it's because I spent my whole life playing sports, dancing, or being an athlete and it was my place where I could go to get emotion out or just be "in the zone" and play and not have to worry about anything else. I really enjoy the balance that it brings to my life and the ability for me to work through things I'm going through. That's just my process. I'm also very competitive and I love pushing myself beyond the limits and seeing what my body can do. I have a lot of fun. It brings me a lot of joy.

Unfortunately, I think a lot of people do stuff that they just don't like. There's a million different ways to work out. That's also why I change a lot of the time...One day I'm doing Pilates, the next day I'm boxing, the next day I'm at the gym lifting. That way I don't get bored and I always have something different to inspire me. My body can do something different, do a different challenge. It's not the same thing every day where I'm thinking, "Well, this sucks. I just have to sweat it out." There are options. I just think that most people don't explore them enough.

For so many of us, it's about getting quiet and asking your body what it needs. This is for food, this is for movement...all of that. What do I need and what do I want? Today, maybe I just want to go for a walk at the beach and that's my movement and fitness for the day. The next day, I might really want to go super hard and the gym and grab a burger because that's what my body is craving. I think we just go through the motions and we just do what everyone else is doing. We don't think about what we want. Being self-aware and knowing how to respond to what your body is asking for is one of the biggest things we miss out on because it's something we're not taught.

KVR: Anything else you'd like to add? Any tips about food or fitness?

KT: The biggest thing I've learned in my healing journey is understanding how food can affect you. It can either be a negative effect and cause brain fog, digestive issues and fatigue...Or it can help clear that and can really nourish your body. Spending the time to get clear on how different foods make you feel and honoring that is really important for so many people on their journeys of being able to appreciate food and what it can do for you. Also, knowing how to utilize it for your body, your performance and your happiness in the best way.

Professional Advice From Fitness Experts & Personal Trainers

Chris "C-Horse" Horstman *chorsefitness.com*

Chris is a fitness specialist & certified personal trainer known for creating highly efficient personalized training programs for all age groups. He is also a former NCAA Division 1 athlete and won the Mountain West Conference championship while playing basketball for San Diego State University, where he graduated with a degree in Kinesiology.

Jason Kozma a.k.a. "Mr. America" *jasonkozma.com*

Jason is a fitness expert and celebrity personal trainer who works with professional athletes to "regular folk" to reach their individual goals. He is also a competitive bodybuilder and has won the following titles: Mr. America, Mr. Muscle Beach, Southern States Champion, Tennessee Valley Champion and Kentucky Derby Champion.

KVR: It's common knowledge that regular exercise is necessary to live a healthy life. What do you tell someone who has a hard time being motivated to work out on a regular basis?

CH: First thing I like to bring up is that there are so many different ways to get exercise. The gym setting is not for everybody, especially being in Southern California, I always suggest some sort of outdoor activity that might be enjoyable for that person. You're able to enjoy some scenery or whatever it may be while getting that exercise.

The other thing is, if we've exhausted all different modes of exercise (boxing, lifting weights, whatever it may be) and they just don't like it, I tell them it's a necessary chore just like washing the dishes or doing your laundry...you don't have to love it, but it has to get done. I try to find ways to help my clients and others to appreciate their bodies and love the process of getting in shape or staying in shape.

I think a lot of people workout because they hate how they look...and if that's their motivation at first then so be it, but work out because you love yourself and you love your body. Do those things out of love, not hate.

JK: I don't have any empathy for that. Just do it, like the Nike commercial. It's a "must do" not a "should do." Nobody does what they should do. They only do what they must do, so working out needs to go in the "must do" category.

KVR: Is it better for the body to have intense workouts with rest days in between, or have lighter workouts every day?

CH: I am of the school of thought that intense full-body workouts with longer rest in between workouts is more beneficial for a couple main reasons: 1) You tax your systems a little harder so you get those signals to your muscles that they have to adapt and grow. 2) Rest is very important. I'm huge on rest. You need good quality sleep to allow those positive changes in your body. During your workout, that's when you break yourself down to a certain extent.

On rest days, I wouldn't say "do nothing." Maybe go for a walk or a light hike because circulation is key. A lot of recovery tools in the industry (e.g. DMS, power plate, vibration technology) all promote greater circulation. The more you get circulation through your body, the faster you can recover and get nutrients where they need to be. There are also cryotherapy places and float tanks to help in recovery. I'm a big fan of ice baths. I'm old fashioned. I've done the cryotherapy, but the ice bath is a little more tortuous and I feel like something's getting done. I'll get four 20-pound bags of ice and fill up my bathtub, usually at the end of my week.

Again, sleep is major for recovery. Something I've been focusing on for myself is staying away from screens late at night and in the morning. I feel like that helps my quality of sleep. I get into those deep sleep REM states that help recovery a lot.

Another benefit to more intense workouts fewer times a week is timing. Not everybody can make it to the gym every day of the week. Working at a gym, I see people so many people work out for an hour, but they're not really pushing themselves. Yeah, it's better than nothing, but if you're not seeing progress after a while, there's a reason for that.

JK: It's definitely better to have more intense workouts with rest days in between.

KVR: In your experience, what are some of the best, most efficient exercises you can do to lose fat and build muscle?

CH: If I had to pick one workout, squatting and pressing in one movement is an exercise I really like. There are a few different ways I have my clients do that. You can do it without weights by squatting and jumping. Or, you can do it with dumbbells, either like a deadlift or a squat by holding the weight between your legs, curling it up and bringing it overhead. The more muscles you get moving and the more of your body you get working, the more energy you're going to expend and the more calories you'll burn.

Another good one is slam balls, the big heavy gym balls. You squat down to pick it up overhead and slam it down as hard as you can, so you're adding a power aspect to it as well.

A lot of bodyweight exercises use your full body already, so those are great. I like primal movements a lot like bear crawls, going across the grass or room in both directions, and what I call "spider crawling," staying as close to the ground as possible and moving forwards and backwards. Breakdancers are another good one, where you have your hands behind you on the floor and you reach your toes on the opposite foot. Pull-ups are one of the #1 strength exercises. It's more of just an arm and back workout. It works out your core really hard as well, if you're doing them properly.

JK: If you're looking for a short answer, there are the basic compound exercises. These include: squats, deadlifts, pullover rows, bench press, overhead press...any exercise that incorporates a lot of muscles.

KVR: In gyms, people tend to either focus on cardio or weight training. Can the body benefit from just sticking to either one or the other, or is it necessary to have some combination of the two? Is there an optimal ratio?

CH: Definitely necessary to have a little of both. Cardio doesn't have to be the traditional idea of cardio where you get on a treadmill or elliptical and run, but you do need to get your heart rate up and get some cardiovascular work done in your workout. Weight lifting or resistance training is imperative. There's no other way to build bone density and strength if you're not bearing some resistance.

The amounts depend on what your goals are. A lot of guys want to put on size and muscle, so they tend to lift more, whereas women tend to do more cardio. A lot of women are worried about getting big and muscular from lifting weights, which is a silly fear because you would have to lift so much weight for so long and take supplements in order for that to happen.

JK: There's definitely a benefit of doing anything over nothing, but it's optimal to do both weights and cardio assuming that your goal is to lose fat and not lose muscle. Most people don't know the difference though. Most people only know that they want to lose weight and don't even think about the muscle. They think that if they train their muscles they'll get huge like me. The fact is, you actually want to lose fat weight and maintain or gain muscle weight. That is what you want, but most people don't understand how the body works.

There's no optimal ratio between cardio and weight training. It depends on the body type of the individual, but you need both because weight training builds muscle and your metabolic rate so your body burns more calories both at rest and when you exercise. So, if you're doing cardio without doing weight training, you're leaving a lot of possible fat-burning components on the table. Weight training doesn't burn body fat at all beyond just elevating the metabolism. You can't do weight training in a way that burns fat because that's not how the body creates energy. The energy created through weight training is anaerobic energy, meaning it's created without the use of oxygen. You can't do weight training in a way that is aerobic. The only way to burn fat is with aerobic exercise and that's basically within a certain heart rate range. It has to be continuous, rhythmic and uses the legs. Things like group circuit training and stuff like that don't really burn fat. They burn calories, which can tangentially add up to some weight loss and some fat loss, but in reality, about half the weight you lose will be muscle and half the weight you lose will be fat. Weight training can either be done effectively, or can easily be done ineffectively. When you try to do weight training a way to burn fat and try to make it into a cardiovascular exercise, it makes it ineffective.

KVR: If you're naturally more into weight-training, what are some of the best cardio exercises to start doing?

CH: I always vouch for things that are low impact like the bike, elliptical and the row machine. Honestly, the rower would probably be the most appealing to guys who are used to lifting weights because there is a strength aspect and it taxes both the upper and lower body if you're doing it right. You get more bang for your buck and get in a really tough workout in ten minutes on the rower. The harder you push yourself on any cardio machine, the more you get out of your workout...But the fact that you're using upper and lower body on the rower, ten minutes is probably more like thirty minutes on any other piece of cardio equipment.

JK: Incline treadmill walking, elliptical machine and stationary bike.

KVR: If you're naturally more into cardio, what are some of the best weight-training exercises to start doing?

CH: I suggest that people get familiar with the machines first. They're a good starting point. If you don't have someone to teach you how to properly brace your spine when lifting, the machines help with that, having a back pad to put your spine in the right position when you're pushing or pulling. Eventually, you want to graduate from the machines because you don't want to rely on that. Every workout, if you're doing it right, should be a core exercise on some level since you're working on keeping that neutral spine. So, I strongly suggest starting with the machines because they're a bit safer, but because the movements are on a track, you'll want to eventually reap the benefits of free weights.

JK: It's the basic exercises that I said before, like squats, deadlifts, pullover rows, bench press and overhead press. But, you really should get some instruction on these doing these properly rather than just going in there and making stuff up.

KVR: Certain types of people avoid the gym because they feel intimidated. What advice do you have for those people?

CH: First thing I would say, as a trainer, is "hire a personal trainer." In any case, don't be afraid to ask questions and talk to the people who work there. Generally speaking, people at the gym aren't afraid to help other people. It looks intimidating and people have their game faces and headphones on, but, for the most part, people are nice and willing to help out if you're a little bit lost. I'd always be wary of their advice, but if you need help moving something or are not sure about how to use something, just ask. I don't see people making fun of anybody. Usually, our fears in our heads are much worse than reality.

JK: Stop making excuses! Gain some basic knowledge. There's tons of free workout apps out there and videos on YouTube that you can learn from. Also, every issue of Muscle and Fitness magazine (which comes out every single month) has pretty good beginner workouts in them. It's not like you can't get some basic knowledge out there prior to stepping foot in the gym. Of course, executing the exercises well does require some in-person coaching.

KVR: Some people don't like going to the gym because they're just not interested in those kinds of repetitive exercises (i.e. lifting weights, running on a treadmill, etc.). Do you have any suggestions for those people?

CH: I'm a big sports guy. I love sports and there's all different levels of sports and different movement requirements in sports. Even at older ages, you can find something that challenges you dynamically and not just physically, but mentally and with your focus. Ping pong is a great way to keep you moving and keep your focus on the ball with your hand-eye coordination. That kind of stuff, where it doesn't feel so repetitive since every point or every play is different and will keep you engaged.

Partner workouts can be fun. Doing something with a friend can help motivate you...and, again, maybe hire a trainer. Part of my training that I really pride myself on is that I want every session to be different and unique. While there may be some drills I might work on with clients over and over to improve, the entire workout as a whole is always going to be different. It keeps people interested and prevents them from thinking it's monotonous and boring. Anybody can find a workout plan, print it out and repeat it every day. As humans, we need some creativity and different stimuli. So hire a good trainer and let them take care of that.

JK: Start to like weight training. I'm not interested in people that say, "I'm not a gym person." I'm definitely not for them. On the other hand, there are many different ways to work out. They can sign up for outdoor boot camp or something like that. At least they would be doing something. It's not as effective as weight training and then doing fat-burning cardio. (There's a difference between doing cardio and doing fat-burning cardio.) But it's much better than doing nothing.

KVR: Breathing is a big part of any physical activity. Do you have any breathing techniques or exercises to help people work out more efficiently?

CH: Great question. I'm a big proponent of the breath, not just in exercise, but in daily life. I meditate, so that's a time of day that I really focus on my breath. Whenever I feel that my equilibrium is off in any way, I try to come back to my breath. I stress that with my clients too. There are some sessions that I start with what I call a "mindful minute" because some people have certain ideas about meditation and religion. I think everyone can practice mindfulness. That minute is just about deep breathing. During workouts, especially when they start to get hard, I remind them to focus on their breath. We always try to aim for slower deeper breaths. Most weightlifting exercises, we do at a slow eccentric (muscle lengthening) tempo. I'll tell them to exhale on the concentric (muscle contracting) part. Connecting your breath with those movements are really helpful.

I don't suggest holding your breath. Some people will do the Valsalva maneuver and try to create as much abdominal pressure as possible to protect their spine, but I'm not a fan of that. Personally, it doesn't feel good for me and I feel like I'm gonna get a hernia, so I don't advise my clients to do that. I always coach to inhale or exhale smoothing throughout movements.

JK: You should usually just breathe naturally. The simplest way to explain it is that you should inhale on the easy part and exhale on the hard part of the exercise.

KVR: What are some common myths about working out that should be busted once and for all?

CH: Well, we touched on one of them...women concerned about getting really buff. That's a major myth.

I think a lot of people have the idea that ab exercises are gonna give you abs. That's a myth also. You'll get a strong core, but if you want your abs to show, it all happens in the kitchen. You have to watch your diet and maybe add more cardio in your workout to trim down.

I don't want to get too into nutrition because that's not my field, but it's a myth that carbs are bad. Certain diets cause more inflammation in the body than others, but you typically want to stick to a balanced diet...Carbs just get a really bad rap.

Stretching before working out is a huge myth. I'm a big believer in a dynamic warm-up (i.e. warming up by moving around a lot). You're taking your muscles close to their end range, but you're not overstretching or holding stretches for long periods. It's a good way to promote circulation and warm your core temperature up and prepare your muscles for exercise. It's not good, in my opinion, to stretch a cold muscle. If you come right into the gym, sit down and start reaching for your toes and holding...that's a recipe for a tear or strain because your muscles are cold and not ready to be extended to that length. So, I like to start with a dynamic warmup before any exercise for all my clients. If there are any areas of their bodies that are extra tight and need static stretching, we do that towards the end of our workouts when the muscles are nice and warm and loose.

JK: Women can't get bulky by accident by doing weight training. Men can't either. It takes years and years and years. It's not like you're going to just wake up one morning and look like me.

Also, muscle can't turn into fat. When you stop training the muscle doesn't turn to fat. It goes away, but most people keep eating the same amount and that's how they put on weight.

KVR: Any other advice you'd like to share about fitness?

CH: I'm a big fan of water in general. Water workouts are awesome: working out in the pool, swimming in the ocean...it's low impact and usually full-body. I love water, you gotta hydrate. Clients will often come to me saying "I have a headache" or "I can't sleep." The first thing I ask is, "Are you drinking enough water?" I don't think many of us realize how much water we should be drinking in a day.

My main mantra as a trainer is, love your body throughout the process and don't do things that you absolutely hate in the gym, but also understand that you don't have to love every single workout. You have to treat it as a chore some days. The days that you don't want to do it and don't feel like doing it, those are the days that make a difference and separate you from your past self or other people who haven't hit their goals. Those are the days you have to bite the bullet and just push through it. You can also adjust your workout too. My favorite is when

I go into the week not having a plan for my workouts. Instead, I base my workouts on however I feel when I get there. If you come into the gym when you're not feeling that hot and you can't finish every workout you wanted to do, that's still better than not showing up...as long as you don't leave the gym in a negative state of mind. Exercise should make you feel good physically and emotionally.

JK: Consistency is the key. You just gotta start, keep going and never stop. Successful people just make it a part of their lifestyle. Unsuccessful people are "two months on, eight months off." It's gotta be part of your life, just like brushing your teeth and taking a shower. Consistency is #1...that's the secret.

Professional Advice From Registered Dietitians & Nutritionists

Cynthia Thurlow, NP

Cynthia is a nurse practitioner, functional nutritionist, certified wellness coach and entrepreneur. She has been featured on TedX and WJLA news segments.

Ilana Muhlstein, MS, RDN

Melissa is a registered dietitian and weight loss expert. She had undergone a 100-pound weight loss transformation and used her personal experience to develop the 2B Mindset™ program, which has helped hundreds of thousands successfully lose weight as well.

Melissa Joy Dobbins, MS, RDN, CDE

Melissa is an award-winning food & nutrition expert and certified diabetes educator. She is also known as The Guilt-Free RD® and the host of the popular Sound Bites® podcast.

KVR: Many people consider themselves to be a certain type of eater (i.e. omnivores, carnivores, pollotarians, pescetarians, vegetarians or vegans). For those who are not omnivores, is it

actually possible to eliminate any one major food group and still be healthy?

CT: I think it gets controversial. People who feel very passionately about or identify with any one particular type of eater, feel that it works for everyone. What I've come to find out as a clinician and as a nutritionist is that ultimately we have to do what agrees with us philosophically as well as physically.

However, I, personally, believe in consuming animal products and that includes meat. I know there are people who vehemently disagree with that. I just know that my body does better with more protein, some plants and healthy fats. I do have many patients that ascribe to a philosophy where they feel that they do best when they are eating a plant-based diet.

This is certainly a hotbed topic. Part of the discussion needs to be that we are always evolving as human beings and, therefore, we need to remain open-minded. What may not make sense to me, may make sense to someone else...and that respect needs to go both ways.

Ultimately, it comes down to: What can you afford? What makes you feel good? If you can eat, sleep and move well; then whatever you're doing is working for you at that period in time. It's as simple as that.

IM: There's not any one type of food anybody needs to eat to survive. There's not one food that's gonna save your life or one food you can't live without from a nutrition perspective. Also, I don't think there's anything anyone needs to focus on cutting out.

It's more about emphasizing what we need to put more of in our system. My trademark is "water first, veggies most." Everyone needs to be focused on these four words that I believe are gonna cure the obesity crazes globally. Everyone needs to drink water first, about 16 oz. prior to their meals and consume veggies most. People get very overwhelmed by that statement of "veggies most," but you don't necessarily need to eat mostly veggies. It can be "veggies some" or "veggies more."

MJD: Eliminating an entire food group is typically not recommended unless someone has an allergy or intolerance. If someone does eliminate a food group they need to be sure to get the nutrients from that food group through other foods or supplements. Oftentimes they will need some guidance from a registered dietitian.

KVR: What is the healthiest way to deal with food cravings and hunger pangs?

CT: Hunger pangs largely don't necessarily mean that you need food. I always remind people that distraction and hydration are things to work on first (if they're purposefully fasting). When it comes to food cravings, it's about checking in with yourself. For example, ask yourself, "Am I getting enough calories per day?" Now, I don't advise anyone to count calories, per se. But, if you're going a week without eating a sufficient amount of calories and you're craving junk, your body might be looking for a quick source of fuel.

There's a difference between someone craving chocolate around their period versus someone who has profound sugar cravings that they can't explain otherwise. That's when diagnostic testing and working with a clinician who's particularly attuned to those kinds of things can be beneficial.

As a rule, it's always: Have you had enough healthy fats? Have you had enough calories during the day? Have you had enough sleep? All of those things can impact your cravings. Also, not all hunger cravings are related to food. It could be psychological...someone looking to feed a feeling they don't want to feel. It could be physiological...they're dehydrated. Just being mindful about hydration is an important key point and can be really beneficial.

IM: The best way to deal with hunger pains is to drink water first because we are always confusing thirst and hunger. We can actually live three weeks without food, but we can't live three days without water...and none of us really drink enough water. Anytime any of us think we're *so* hungry or, God-forbid "starving" (I hate that word and don't normally use it), it's usually because you need to be drinking water first. That already presents the feeling of fullness and satisfaction and helps people to make healthier choices later on.

MJD: Eating on a regular schedule and not skipping meals is the best way to manage or prevent hunger and cravings.

KVR: There are plenty of buzz words in food these days (e.g. organic, natural, non-GMO, gluten-free, nightshades, etc.). Which of these terms should people actually pay attention to?

CT: This is a great question. I believe there is value to paying attention to whether or not something is organic. There are two great resources updated yearly by Environmental Working Group: The Dirty Dozen and The Clean Fifteen. The ones listed on The Dirty Dozen are worth buying organic. We don't have to buy *everything* organic, but quality is important because pesticide exposure can reap a lot of negative impact on our bodies.

"Natural" and "natural flavors" mean nothing. There's no way to tell exactly what it means. That's a marketing scheme. Buyer beware.

Gluten-free can be a marketing gimmick, but it's also beneficial for people who have Celiac disease (or don't have Celiac disease, but may do better without it) to exclude gluten from their diet and to be able to look at a food label and know that there's no gluten products in there. It becomes problematic because you get so much gluten exposure from different types of grains.

Many people are unfamiliar with nightshades and the concept that there are a group of plants (tomatoes, potatoes, eggplants, etc.) that can induce inflammation in the body and cause pain or non-restful sleep. We know that can be a key inflammatory food group. So, it can be beneficial to pull them out to see if your sleep is better, your digestion is better, your pain is better. If I, personally, have too many tomatoes at this point in my life, I will get plantar fasciitis pain in my right foot...almost always.

IM: That's a great point. It's all a matter of the person's personality. If you're a balanced person and you have a reasonable approach to weight loss and health because you had positive role models (for example: your parents showed balance and you were able to discover it), then having organic vegetables when possible isn't a bad thing. However, when people aren't balanced in their approach and become too crazed and obsessed over something like organic vegetables, then they think it's not even worth eating vegetables when it's not organic. That's where the issue lies. They think "Ugh, these organic vegetables are so expensive," so then they end up getting Popeye's. I'm about not bringing any stigma to any food because every veggie is better than having none at all, even if it's doused with mayonnaise and croutons. I believe that the more stigma has grown around food, the worse our health has gotten.

MJD: Instead of buzzwords, I encourage people to focus on "nutrient-rich foods" – to eat foods that provide a lot of nutrients to increase (like fiber, calcium) compared to nutrients to avoid in excess (like calories, saturated fat, sodium). Those buzzwords or label "claims" do not necessarily indicate "healthy" – an organic, natural, gluten-free cookie is still a cookie.

KVR: Is it generally better for the body to eat completely healthy on most days and have the occasional "cheat day," or eat healthy every day and also allow yourself a less-healthy treat every day?

CT: I intrinsically believe in the power of food. So I think moderation, not deprivation, is better. 80% of the time, you should be eating healthfully and for the other 20% have a cheat meal, not a cheat day. I find that when people do a cheat day, they go completely overboard and they will go from eating fairly healthy to all of a sudden going on a binge and they can't go back. I find that there is value in prioritizing the quality of the foods you're putting in your body consistently. Teenagers and 20-year-olds can get away with a whole lot more than people, say, north of 35 can. A lot of the patients that I encounter can't eat the way they did when they were 18. Not only is it the quality, but the quantity of food can be much more of an issue.

IM: I coined the term "treat not cheat." So, I definitely don't believe in a cheat day as much as I believe in allowing yourself some freedom throughout the week. The problem is that, first of all, when people say "cheat," nothing positive is associated with that word. "Cheating" is completely surrounded by the premise of guilt and wrongdoing. You can't fully enjoy something and indulge in a positive experience if you think it's the wrong thing to be doing. I always recommend that people use the word "treat" and not "cheat." When people use the word "treat," they can actually feel good about it. They actually enjoy the food more and it doesn't take as much to solve for the craving that they're experiencing. I've actually never seen a client enjoy a treat and gain weight, but if they're eating banana bread from the bottom of a container because they feel like they've already cheated, then they can gain lots of weight.

A really good sample day of a client whom I recently met went on the scale one day and when she went on the scale the next day, she saw that she had lost a pound. I call that a "weight loss" day. For breakfast, she had Starbucks' sous vide egg white bites. For lunch, she had a big grilled chicken sandwich. Then later in the afternoon, she had two handfuls of popcorn and a Dove chocolate. For dinner, she had frozen zucchini noodles and meatballs. I look at that as a big win because this is someone who used to not be able to have chocolate and popcorn without the guilt. She was able to lose weight in a day because she was focused on eating lots of vegetables and having protein at every meal, things that allow you to have self-control around these treats. If you fill up on "water first" and "veggies most," you have a much stronger sense of self-control vs. starting your day with a donut and having sugar crashes and spikes all day. It's not good from an inflammation standpoint, a diabetes prevention standpoint, for your heart and mindset...plus you'll feel sluggish that day. It's just not a good idea. After a decent meal of, for example, roasted vegetables and chicken or salmon, even if you have a snack like chocolate-covered almonds, it's a lot harder to overeat. When you have a cheat meal and start with a burger and fries, it's been shown that you don't just eat more sugar and carbs, but you tend to eat more overall, so everything is just working against you from the viewpoint of wanting to be able to stop.

MJD: It's important to eat healthy foods but it's also important to have a healthy "relationship" with food. By setting up a "cheat" day you are setting up a good vs. bad approach which can be problematic.

It's best to aim for healthy choices and behaviors overall, allowing yourself small indulgences along the way.

KVR: Many people seem to follow fad diets whether it's the Atkins diet or keto diet. Are there actually any diets out there that actually work long-term?

CT: I'm of the philosophy that we, as a society, as a whole need to eat less processed, more nutrient-dense foods. Some of what I recommend may fall into a little bit of each of those camps. There are reasons why these diets become popular; people are looking for alternatives. Many people are finding that a standard American diet is not working for them: they're obese, they're diabetic, they're insulin-resistant, they're hypertensive, their cholesterol is down the toilet, and they're dealing with infertility and a multiplicity of other things.

For the most part, when people really focus on less-processed foods, *that's* what's really at the core of many of these diets...less processed foods. That is something that I think can be transitional and not trendy. My hope is that that's what people will take away from those philosophies.

IM: My program, called the 2B Mindset™, has been designed to be simple, sensible and, most importantly, sustainable. I think there are hundreds of thousands (if not millions) of ways a person could lose weight and I have no ego about that. It's the piece on sustainability that I think I've solved for effectively. A big approach to that is 1) I never focus on what someone is not doing, it's always a positive focus so you actually feel good about yourself along the way. There's no way to cheat using my program. You're only cheating yourself if you don't write the food down or all these other things I would recommend. I've designed this whole process around sustainability because I've lost a hundred pounds and I've kept it off even after having two children. From my perspective, prior to creating my program, I would lose weight and gain it. I was so sick of doing this a million times, so I like to cater to the person who is fed up gaining weight back.

With keto, people gain weight back really quickly because you're really depleting your muscle mass and you're messing with your whole metabolic pathway. So, I don't recommend that. A lot of these programs will work until they don't. The problem is that people beat themselves up for gaining that weight back from unsustainable systems. That, for me, is the saddest piece...that people blame themselves for not having a stronger sense of self-control, but they're doing things that are designed for you to not have self-control. Someone who's smoking cigarettes won't feel so defeated for having a hard time quitting because the addictive nature of cigarettes is so well known. Unfortunately, as much as we study these different diets, people don't like to admit that the programs they're using are not sustainable. People just like to worship whoever designed it and try to hang on to whatever phony science that person presented in their book, then beat themselves up for not having that self-control.

MJD: The only diet that works long term is the one you can stick with. Otherwise, you lose the weight and regain it when you go back to your regular diet. Most people find it difficult to stick with extreme diets like these but some people are able to. If you're able to stick with an extreme diet you may be missing out on important nutrients such as fiber, vitamins, minerals.

KVR: There are a wide variety of salts used in food these days (e.g. iodized salt, kosher salt, sea salt, pink Himalayan salt, etc.). Are there certain salts that are actually healthier than others, or should they all be used sparingly?

CT: When I think of processed salt, I think of iodized salt which used to serve the purpose of preventing goiter. When I think of kosher salt, sea salt, pink Himalayan salt...those have key minerals and tend to be stronger so people tend to use less of them. They're much more flavorful, so I do believe there is a distinctive difference. Himalayan salt has over 70 key minerals that you wouldn't otherwise get in your diet, especially from iodized salt since it's super processed. Let the buyer beware. Most of what you find in restaurants and served in public places is iodized salt, which hardly has any nutritional value at all. Limiting those kinds of varieties would be hugely beneficial.

IM: We know that sugar salt and fat is addictive, so I'm a big fan of finding ways to add sugar, salt and fat to veggies. What happens is that people say, "I need to stop eating sugar, salt and fat in other foods, so I should just eat steamed kale and eat it plain," but that doesn't work because it doesn't taste good. Instead, when you add some salt and a little bit of caramelized pecans over green beans, you end up eating a lot more green beans.

Sea salt and pink Himalayan salt has definitely been shown to be more dense in minerals, which is great and not as processed with anti-caking agents and things like that. Interesting enough, we know our #1 source of salt is from restaurant foods; it's not in our own cooking. A lot of people are afraid to add salt to their own food, but then they don't make tasty food, so they end up eating at more restaurants. If you add some salt to your meals, it's usually ok.

MJD: All salts are the same when it comes to sodium content. However, what most people don't realize is that most of the salt/sodium in our diets is already in the food (either naturally occurring or through processing – which helps with food safety/shelf life in addition to flavor). So any salt we "add" to foods is above and beyond that and probably means we are getting more than we need. However, sodium is typically not the most important concern in most people's diets. Most people are lacking in fruits, vegetables and fiber and should focus on getting more of those before looking at their sodium intake.

KVR: There are also a wide variety of sweeteners used in food these days (e.g. cane sugar, brown sugar, stevia, agave, honey, monk fruit, etc.). Are there certain salts that are actually healthier than others, or should they all be used sparingly?

CT: If anyone's going to consume a sweetener, I would recommend and prefer that they consume something more natural and like raw locally sourced honey. If they have a stevia plant or organic stevia drops, that's certainly better than the garbage Coca-Cola puts out called Truvia. I'm not a fan of artificial sweeteners. It's not the way our bodies are designed to eat. Quality matters.

When comes to sugar, when it so proliferates in our food anyway, I believe it should always be limited. But, if you need to add a sweetener to something, finding something that's more natural like molasses, the stevia plant, raw locally sourced honey...those are definitely better options.

One sweetener that drives me crazy is agave, which was really hot several years ago. Unfortunately, that spikes your insulin just like having an injection of fructose. It's a terrible alternative. Pure maple syrup is much better.

Then you start delineating that fructose, which is frowned upon, is found in fruits. The thing is, fresh fruits naturally contain beneficial vitamins and fiber, which lowers the absorption of fructose. I think many people are confused. That's one of the greatest challenges of all is that people are desperate for good information and yet there is so much misinformation out there.

IM: I classify sweeteners in a few different ways. There are caloric sweeteners which can either be natural and unnatural. The natural caloric sweeteners are: honey, agave, coconut sugar and maple syrup. They all have about 15-20 calories per teaspoon and raise your blood sugar level. Yes, they are healthier than unnatural calorie ones, but they still raise your blood sugar levels, contain calories and can lead to obesity and diabetes when overused. The unnatural caloric sweetener that no one should have is high fructose corn syrup. I definitely recommend that everyone reads labels to make sure they're not consuming things with high fructose corn syrup. But again, if you're in the middle of nowhere having barbecue and you eat two pieces of grilled chicken and some veggies with a teaspoon or two of BBQ sauce that has high fructose corn syrup, that's better than having the white bun and some s'mores and all these other things. In the end, I do recommend people avoid high fructose corn syrup as much as possible.

I definitely add sweeteners like honey and coconut sugar to my salad dressings and marinades to make veggie stir-fries. I call these things "accessories," so anything that gets you to eat more veggies is a good thing. When people make homemade lemonade with cups and cups of sugar or maple syrup, or they make a "healthier dessert" which is just a ton of dates with almond butter and they can't stop eating it so they overeat as a result, that's not actually healthy.

Then there are zero-calorie sweeteners. The artificial ones are: acesulfame K, sucralose, aspartame, Equal and Splenda. I recommend that people avoid as much as possible because they are so much sweeter than sugar and I find that they make it hard for people to control their sweet cravings. We are starting to see research that they are also unhealthy for gut health, that they are potentially harmful to your gut bacteria. The last group are the natural zero-calorie sweeteners: stevia, monk fruit and erythritol (i.e. sugar alcohol). I'm actually okay with those. I love stevia and I've done a lot of research on stevia and it's been used for centuries, even for medicinal properties, so I think it's fine. I consume it daily in my coffee and my tea, so I'm fine recommending that my clients have it.

MJD: All "sugars" are still sugar and all approved nonnutritive sweeteners ("artificial" sweeteners) are safe and are an option for people who want to decrease or manage their sugar and/or added sugar intake.

KVR: Flavored sparkling water has become a popular replacement for soda over recent years. Is that actually good for your health?

CT: Well, if someone's drinking soda and they switch to flavored sparkling water, that's going to be better than drinking soda. But if you ask, "What's the best thing to drink?" I would say that, ideally, you should drink filtered water and squeeze some lemon or lime in it. Other good alternatives are green tea, or plain coffee. But, it's good, better, best. That's always what it comes back to.

When you start looking at "natural flavors" that I see on the sides of cans and bottles, it makes me bananas because these manufacturers don't have to disclose what's in it. It's probably some kind of sugar. That's a good way to dismantle a lot of good work you've done in taking care of your body. Liquid calories are a huge problem, not just in the United States, but outside the United States as well.

Some people try to drink water and say "But it doesn't taste like anything!" Well, it's not intended to. Our palates have gotten incredibly conditioned to consuming sweet things. That's where the trouble lies. Unfortunately, physicians don't talk to their patients about drinking water. It's never been a priority, but it's foundational to our health. You've got to sleep and you gotta drink water. It's important that people recognize that their fatigue is not just because they ate a crappy meal, but usually because they are dehydrated. You really need to be attuned to your body.

IM: Yes, very much for many reasons. Artificial colors are actually banned in other countries. One nice thing about sparkling waters is that they are colorless. A Diet Coke adds caramel coloring for no other reason than aesthetic purposes. If you're drinking it from a can, why would you even want to be staining your teeth? Also, most sparkling waters don't use artificial sweeteners, but again, you'll have to look at the label to check on that because some of them do. The main benefit to sparkling water is that the first ingredient is actually water and is a way of hydrating yourself, plus they're usually calorie-free. One of the biggest causes of obesity is the consumption of sugar-sweetened beverages and high-calorie beverages from juices to sodas. I just saw a 15-year-old girl buy something like a 20-ounce can of iced tea with about 300 calories in it and drink it mindlessly, so calorie-containing beverages are a *huge* issue. I think people can get too focused on "water is better," but sparkling water is way better than what they're currently drinking.

KVR: The importance of gut bacteria or gut flora is also growing in popularity. What's your opinion on gut bacteria and what are some foods that people can eat or avoid to make sure they have a healthy gut?

CT: That's a great question. First and foremost, processed foods, excitotoxins, artificial dyes and colors are not good for our gut flora. I always say that you want to go back to the basics: probiotic-rich foods like fermented vegetables (Wildbrine makes a great variety), full-fat organic dairy (preferably unsweetened) or coconut milk yogurt (like The Coconut Collaborative), low-sugar kombucha, wild-brine olives...these probiotic-rich foods are always a great choice. Having a lot of variety in protein sources and healthy fats are really critical. The health of our gut bacteria is really important. The bulk of our neurotransmitters are produced in our gut—75-80% of our neurotransmitters that are our "feel-good" hormones or anxiety-producing hormones are produced in the gut. Sometimes when people do an elimination diet and pull out gluten or dairy, all of a sudden their depression or anxiety goes away. I think a variety of foods, probiotic-rich foods, are certainly critical.

Also, stress plays a huge role in our gut bacteria, making sure that your stress is dialed-in...as simplistic as it sounds. It's our enteric second brain. You know that jittery, nervous stomach feeling that people get? There's a strong correlation with what they're perceiving as a stressor and what their gut picks up on, which can really be critical.

Another piece of that is that there's no food monogamy. You're not eating the same thing for breakfast, lunch and dinner every single day...and a lot of people are that way. The body needs variety.

IM: People will focus on probiotic-rich foods like sauerkraut, yogurt and kefir. But in my opinion, it can be way more beneficial to focus on prebiotic foods. Prebiotics are the food that feeds the good bacteria in your gut. There's a lot of support and research showing that when you take probiotic supplements, a lot of them are dead by the time they hit your colon. We have existing good bacteria in our gut and if you feed it the food it wants, these prebiotics, then they can grow and proliferate. The best way to do this is by eating vegetables, high fiber vegetables like artichokes, asparagus, mushrooms...those are all really good.

KVR: What are some common myths about eating that should be busted once and for all?

CT: Too many women feel guilt about food. They feel guilty about how much they eat. They feel guilty about what they eat...and the fact that they aren't the same size that they were at sixteen-years-old. I always feel like the guilt about food is hugely problematic. You should just enjoy what you're eating at let it be. Let it go. Give yourself permission to let go of those constraints and restrictions we've imposed upon ourselves about certain types of foods. If you have a piece of cake, enjoy it. If you have two glasses of wine, enjoy it. It just isn't healthy to walk around with food guilt. That's why we have these extremes with anorexia, bulimia and binge eating. It's a reaction and response to people having this poor internal dialogue with themselves. It's a way of punishing themselves in many ways, or having more control over their lives.

I think that there's a perception that you can out-exercise a crappy diet. Now, I'm not picking on CrossFitters...every type of movement is great. I'm just using this as an example. CrossFit is a very intense exercise, but if you think you can do CrossFit and eat McDonald's 3x a day, you're doing your body a complete disservice. You can't out-exercise a crappy diet.

I don't believe in counting calories. The whole concept of calories is, pardon me, bullshit.

Antiquated dogma that breakfast is the most important meal of the day...That's another one that drives me absolutely crazy. A lot of the stuff that I was schooled in when I was doing my training is largely disproven at this point.

IM: One myth is that chemicals are bad, so people have become scared of chemicals. Water is technically a chemical, H_2O. People use that term over and over again without really knowing what it means.

A big myth people have is that if you cook vegetables, it kills all the nutrients. Vegetables are jam-packed with nutrients. If you were to boil broccoli you might lose about 15% of Vitamin C off the top. But if you add some butter to it and end up eating three cups of broccoli vs. barely being able to stomach half a cup or raw broccoli, then you're going to be more than making up for that nutrient loss just due to the fact that you're making it taste more delicious.

I have a hard time when someone tells me that they are a "sugar addict" or a "food addict." I understand OA (Overeaters Anonymous) has helped a lot of people and there's a book called *Bright Line Eating* which is very similar and tells people that they're all addicts. I also feel like I used to be an addict, but I have created a system and program that actually gives you self-control around different foods. It's a fact that some of these foods are addictive. Pringles' slogan is "Once you pop, you can't stop," so why are you beating yourself up for not being able to stop? They have literally engineered the product to prove that point. A big myth that I'd like to debunk is that people have no self-control around food. I just think they need to learn a better approach in order to foster a better sense of self-control with food.

Lastly, a really big myth is that people think they can't lose weight because they have a bad metabolism. *I* have a really bad metabolism. *I* have the obese genes and things like that. At the end of the day, our obesity levels have pretty much doubled in the last forty years. So, somehow we're all saying we have bad genes when people in our family just twenty years ago were not obese. There's really so much more you *can* do. It's that victim mentality that I'd like to debunk because it *is* possible to lose weight whatever your genes are.

KVR: There's a lot of food information out there, especially on the internet, yet many people still struggle to make the right food choices. Any other advice or tips about food or eating that can help people make the right decisions?

CT: Yeah, keep a food diary. It sounds a little simplistic, but there's a lot of correlation between what you eat and how you feel. Like food and mood...Did you eat a meal and feel like you had energy, or did you eat a meal and feel like you had to take a nap? Do you have a daily bowel movement? We are supposed to poop every day and people don't even want to talk about it. It's like they're humiliated and don't even want to have this discussion. Listen, everyone does it. You gotta think about those things. It's not normal to poop once a week. So yeah, keeping a food diary will give you some perspective. Keep it for a week.

We shouldn't be passive conduits to food. We should take an active interest, even if we make something very simple at home. We should learn how to cook. We should learn to go to the grocery store and buy real food, not buy something in a box, bag or can...*real* food. We have gotten so separated from the whole construct of creating meals. Get to know your farmer's markets. There are very few people that I know who don't have access to a farmer's market or co-op. Actually talk to the people growing and preparing their food. Ask them real questions.

Lastly, just enjoy food. We think of food as a means to an end. We're missing the whole point. Just travel outside of the United States. I'll use Spain as an example. I love the food in Spain, the people in Spain, the culture...They savor food. On the other hand, we, as Americans, are in a rush all the time. Digestion starts in our brains. If you're stressed, if you're running around, if you're not connected to what you're doing, you're out of your body...you're not going to digest your food properly. Is it any wonder that we have these multi-million dollar businesses for antacids and reflux medications? People are just throwing food down their throats as they're driving in their cars, standing up at work and looking after their kids. No one sits for meals. No one relaxes. One time a day, just sit down and enjoy a meal.

IM: Honestly, I would really recommend people to get my program. I include every single secret that I've uncovered from my private clients, myself and all my research. Outside of being a Registered Dietitian, UCLA hired me to do a 12-week weight-loss seminar for 100 employees for ten semesters. Those 1,000 people covered all different demographics and were from all walks of life, janitors to chefs and everyone from 25-year-olds to 65-year-olds. My seminar brought the average weight-loss from 12 pounds in 12 weeks to 24 pounds in 12 weeks. I really worked off of that to create my method. I'm not quiet about my advice. I want everyone to get healthier.

I have four core principles, which I call my "two bunnies" because when you put your fingers up they look like bunnies. I mentioned the first two earlier, "water first, veggies most." So, again, always drink 16 ounces of water before you eat and really try to eat more vegetables. A lot of people cringe at that, but just eat more vegetables than you're eating now. You could try to eat 1 cup of vegetables by 1 p.m., which would be 6 baby carrots or 1 sliced bell pepper. It can really make a huge difference. They could be sautéed or dipped in ranch to make it taste better. Definitely eat more vegetables since it has been proven over and over and over again to be beneficial for weight loss. My third core principle is to use the scale. I'm a big, big fan of the scale and I have a lot of research proving its effectiveness for sustainable weight loss. When people who are trying to lose weight avoid the scale, they're often gaining immense amounts of weight. And I'm a big proponent of tracking your food, which is my fourth core principle. One of the only reasons why calorie counting and Weight Watchers apps work is just that they get people to write down their food, which has been proven over and over again to help with weight loss. My program explains all the details of how to follow all these core principles successfully.

MJD: By focusing on nutrient-rich foods (foods that provide important nutrients that our bodies need) and limiting "empty calorie foods" (foods that don't provide much nutrition but have a lot of calories) you can avoid a lot of the confusion and hype about diets. Nearly everyone needs more fruits, vegetables and fiber so that's how you can make a huge difference and improvement in your diet. In addition, many people think that fruits and vegetables must be fresh (or even organic) in order to "count" or to be healthy – but that's not true. Fresh, frozen, canned, dried and juices are all good choices for fruits and vegetables. Not only will that help save you money, it also helps reduce food waste.

MJD (bonus tip): In regards to feeding the hungry, my daughter and I go to our farmer's market and pick up fresh produce donations from farmers to bring to our community's food pantry.

RELATIONSHIPS

When I was a teenaged freshman living in the dorms at UCSD, one of the neighboring suites hosted a movie night for all the students on our floor. The selected feature was a childhood favorite of mine, *Spaceballs*, so I couldn't miss it. (Yes, I mentioned disliking Pizza the Hutt in the early part of this book, but as a fan of satirical and parodic films, I had always thought this Mel Brooks piece was stellar.)

The movie had yet to start when I arrived, but pretty much all the seats and floor space were already taken. Being the kind of person who relishes getting the #1 parking space in any busy parking lot, I walked by the tiny crowded area of prime real estate to see if anyone had overlooked a primo seat. Luckily, one of the guys who lived on the other side of the suite, Robert, whom I had recently met on the elevator, said there was room for me on the giant red beanbag where he was sitting. Although *Spaceballs* was entertaining as always, the nightlong conversation Robert and I shared afterward turned out to be far more captivating. Little did I know that this 18-year-old boy would one day be my husband.

Many teenage love stories end before they ever really get started. Fortunately for Robert and me, ours persisted. On paper, the odds were against us. We grew up with very different backgrounds. I was raised Catholic and he was raised Jewish. I attended private schools from preschool through high school and he went to public school. I was a very adventurous eater and he was a hamburger-and-hot-dog guy. Our differences made for interesting discussions and debates. They also led to many growing pains in the early days of our relationship.

However, because Robert and I shared active lifestyles, had similar life goals, remained open-minded and had a strong mutual love and respect for each other, we've been able to build an indestructible foundation for our relationship over the years, which has turned into a lasting (and very happy) marriage.

As with the evolution of my eating habits throughout my life, Robert and I have greatly evolved as a couple through our life experiences together. And, in the same way my eating habits have become effortless, our marriage has become relatively effortless as well. Don't get me wrong. As a lifelong commitment, marriage requires plenty of work and attention. But when you're happy to do what's necessary to keep a strong marriage going, it doesn't feel like work. Although we still have differences of opinions, they're not an excuse for marital arguments. In fact, we hardly ever argue. We have greatly matured since we were teens and now we know what works for us.

Still, we remain true to ourselves as individuals. It's not like Robert has switched from eating burgers and hot dogs—which I have nothing against and occasionally partake in eating as well—to strictly eating rare and exotic dishes. Instead, he has developed a greater appreciation for the broader food world and respects my penchant for foods less known in the United States. He supportively accompanies me on "food explorations" to fulfill my curiosity, often discovering a dish or two he genuinely likes. Whether in the realm of food or in other areas, we make our relationship work. If we had let our contrasting pasts determine our future, our relationship never would have flourished. Like all human beings, we are much more than our origins. Whatever you're trying to achieve, your past does not control you. Your goals, actions and determination are much more important in shaping your future.

The success of my relationship with Robert can also be attributed to the many admirably healthy relationships that have surrounded us. Making good, responsible decisions is easy when everyone around you is making good, responsible decisions as well. The motivational speaker John Rohm is credited with saying that you are the average of the five people you spend the most time with. It turns out there is scientific evidence—at least related to health—that many more people than you may realize influence who you are. According to a study on

"Spread of Obesity in a Large Social Network over 32 Years" published by the *New England Journal of Medicine*, if your friend is obese, you're 45% more likely to gain weight over the next few years than random chance would predict. If your friend's friend is obese, you are 20% more likely to gain weight, even if you've never met that person. If a friend of your friend's friend is obese you are 10% more likely to gain weight, again, even if you've never met that person. This research suggests that, to reach your goals, you should build strong relationships with people who support your path, share your path or have successfully gone down your path.

Food is an important part of a balanced diet.

-Fran Lebowitz

Like all good relationships, your relationship with food can succeed only if you give it proper attention. In other words, you must be present with your food. Eat mindfully. Be fully conscious and aware of what you're putting in your mouth. When people don't pay attention to what they're eating, the amount of food they perceive to have eaten is often inaccurate.

One common example of not eating mindfully is eating while you are distracted. Eating while watching TV, browsing social media or working at your desk makes it easy to mindlessly put food in your mouth without realizing how much you've actually consumed. Just as it's hard to nurture a healthy relationship with a friend or significant other while you're checking email and social media, you can't maintain a healthy relationship to eating if you're not giving it your full attention. Eating is a full experience in and of itself, no matter what kind of food you're consuming. When you pay attention, you can learn something—even from awful meals, like how to make the experience better next time or remembering not to eat a particular food again.

Another example of not eating mindfully is eating too quickly. Slow down and savor your food. Not only will you have a more fulfilling eating experience and avoid indigestion, but less food will be required to satiate your hunger. If you find yourself really hungry or short on time, you may scarf down your food within a few minutes. Then you might still feel hungry—even though you've eaten everything on your plate. Instead of eating more, drink some water and wait 20 to 30 minutes. That allows time for your brain to receive the signal that you're full. The exploitation of this scientific fact is a primary reason why the competitive eaters at Coney Island can eat so many hot dogs; they eat incredibly fast, inhaling as much food as humanly possible before they start feeling full. Unless you are a trained professional preparing for an eating competition yourself, do the opposite: take your time to appreciate each bite. Your taste buds, digestive system and the rest of your body will thank you.

The third, and one of the most prevalent examples, of not eating mindfully is being stuck in a routine that isn't customized to your personal needs. Society has structured our food intake into meals: breakfast, lunch and dinner with snacks in between. Our bodies get used to this routine, which is instilled in us at an early age through school and later at work. Although this structure may work for some, it doesn't work for everyone. Plenty of people require less food, while others require more. When we are conditioned to follow a certain eating routine, our bodies feel hungry at certain times because they are programmed to do so, even when we may not require more food. Always drink water to stay well-hydrated and ensure that the hunger you may feel isn't thirst in disguise. Listen closely to how *your* body feels. Eat *when* it's necessary for you and *how much* is necessary for you. You're not required to eat a full plate of food just because it's dinner time. Mindfulness is the key to any healthy relationship, especially with food.

Depending on where your interests lie, your relationship with fitness and exercise may prove to be easier or more challenging than your relationship with food. Those who enjoy playing sports or being physically active already have a good foundation for fitness because correlating physical activity with feeling good makes a workout routine more sustainable. Those on the other end of the spectrum, who gravitate toward a more sedentary lifestyle, need to discover a physical activity they can look forward to doing regularly.

This wiseness of finding a physical activity that interests you is based on the concept underlying the popular quote commonly credited to Confucius: "Do what you love and you'll never work a day in your life." This quote is commonly misinterpreted as "hard work isn't necessary when you find something that you love." The truth is, every area of life where you want to make significant improvements requires hard work. Anything truly life-changing is difficult before it gets easier. You have to accept that there will be challenging days ahead and commit to the process despite those days.

If your goal is to improve your relationship with your significant other, you have to put in the hard work of maintaining constant clear communication while controlling your emotions to learn how to deal effectively with different situations as they arise. If you want to improve your eating habits to be healthier, you have to put in the hard work of figuring out what style of eating works best for your body and making those habits a part of your lifestyle. If you want to build a stronger body, you have to put in the hard work of constantly challenging your body and mind through some form of sustainable exercise until that also becomes part of your lifestyle. You must let go of all your excuses.

Technically, I am allergic to exercise. I have been medically diagnosed with exercise-induced bronchoconstriction, commonly known as exercise-induced asthma. During strenuous exercise (especially in cold air), my airways constrict and my body produces excess mucus in my nasal passages, making it difficult to breathe. I pretty much have a "doctor's note for life" excusing me from intense workouts. Do I let that stop me from doing any physical activity? No. In fact, I engage in some form of intense physical activity most days each week, which has reduced the severity of my symptoms. Challenging myself through many different forms of activity, whether golf or indoor rock climbing, improves my strength and skills. Challenging myself is also fun and makes me feel good.

Your love and understanding of the greater purpose and, ideally, the underlying process, makes the hard work doable day in and day out. Stick with the process and your mind and body will undoubtedly get stronger. Whatever you are doing will feel easier and your goals will be more achievable. You'll know you've achieved a healthy relationship with fitness when you feel the need to exercise regularly and feel off without it.

The most important relationship you'll ever have is the one you have with yourself. *Everything* in your life depends on how you view and treat yourself. If you don't value yourself, treat yourself well or believe you are worthy of self-respect, guess what? Your relationship with yourself (i.e., *you*) will completely fall apart. Although we've uncovered several key points necessary in successful relationships, the common denominator among those points is good-quality knowledge of yourself.

Knowing yourself is the beginning of all wisdom.

-Aristotle

Know yourself. Understand everything you possibly can about yourself, inside and out: your mind, your body, your personality—all of it. This self-knowledge is essential for making decisions and taking actions that are most beneficial for you.

I've unearthed countless aspects of myself over the decades. To illustrate how the process of knowing yourself can help your relationship with food, I'll share a few of the idiosyncrasies that have worked for my eating habits. Some make my food a bit healthier.

Others satisfy my outrageously adventurous palate. And all of them make my personal eating experience much more enjoyable.

Most of my friends think my eating habits are a tad eccentric. Even my husband, Robert, thinks some of these quirks are incredibly bizarre. But I've gotta be me!

Some of my unconventional food-related habits include:

- not eating cheese on pizza (which, as you know, stemmed from my childhood)
- brushing excess salt off of tortilla chips with my clean fingers
- adding a few drops of tempura dipping sauce to my scrambled eggs instead of salt
- adding hot sauce and/or hot peppers to nearly all the savory dishes I eat
- putting ice cubes in my cold cereal (back when I used to eat cereal for dessert) because I wanted it to be ice cold to the last spoonful
- not drinking coffee or beer because I can detect even the slightest soupçon of bitterness
- eating around the chocolate chips in chocolate chip cookies
- eating dark chocolate (and sometimes white chocolate or ruby chocolate), but not milk chocolate

- eating every item on my plate in even proportions because I like to enjoy a variety of flavors through the entirety of my meals
- modifying the basic In-N-Out burger to my exact specifications, which In-N-Out employees take great pride in getting right the first time (i.e. a hamburger, mustard-fried, no pickles, whole grilled onions, chopped chilies and extra toast)
- frequently ordering the most unusual item on the menu including, but not limited to: *balut* (fertilized duck egg), *dinuguan* (pig's blood stew), crickets, offal (organ meats), raw tamilok (woodworms), Rocky Mountain oysters (bull testicles), and *shirako* (cod sperm)
- photographing most dishes I eat for my personal records and not for social media

As I suggest everyone does, I have adapted my eating style around my individual lifestyle and schedule. My mind normally becomes hyperactive at night, which is when I get much of my work done. I routinely stay up after midnight. I aim to get seven to eight hours of quality sleep a night, so I'm normally up around 8:30 a.m. (my optimal wake-up time according to the DNA test I took, is). My hunger doesn't usually kick in until noon. Until then, I only drink water to remain hydrated. Once noon hits, I have my first meal and eat as much as I want until midnight. It took a bit of trial and error to figure out that eating within a 12-hour window was ideal for me. I used to eat during traditional mealtimes, but I often felt bloated and overcome with lethargy during the afternoon.

When Robert began intermittent fasting one summer to shed ten superfluous pounds and get back his goal weight, he ate only between the hours of 2 p.m. and 10 p.m. It worked wonders for him; he has maintained that eating schedule and his ideal weight ever since. However, because he and I would regularly eat together, I ate within that same 8-hour window. I didn't realize that his slimming tactic was working for me as well—I also was losing weight. I involuntarily lost several pounds over the course of a month and dropped below my ideal weight. To regain my lost pounds, I expanded my eating window to my current half-day schedule with zero food restrictions.

Although I don't limit my food intake in any way, I feel my best—focused, energetic, healthy and happy—when I drink primarily water and eat a wide variety of foods. I avoid too much of any one type of food because when I overindulge I feel unbalanced, which is most apparent when I eat red meat too frequently. I usually opt for poultry, fish and vegetables over red meat—unless the meat is of high quality, is an ingredient in a unique dish that I have yet to experience or I simply haven't had it in weeks.

This method of eating, in conjunction with living a varied and active lifestyle, has proven effective in maintaining optimal health, which I judge based on how I feel and on regular medical tests. I've spent time deciphering various aspects of myself because I truly value myself. The result—my health and happiness—has been worth the effort.

Think of yourself as a one-of-a-kind puzzle that you alone must solve. Others can provide hints and guides, or sometimes even share their solutions, but it's up to you to execute the best steps to *your* solution (i.e., your desired levels of health and happiness). The right solution will be sustainable and easy to replicate with practice. I've had tons of practice since I first solved my own puzzle. Now I can solve it backwards, forwards and with my eyes closed. I've learned more efficient ways to solve it. I have become the master of figuring out what works for me, integrating those practices into my lifestyle and following them until the process has become effortless.

Certain general truths *do* apply to everyone. Two of these are *eat healthily* and *exercise regularly*. However, healthful eating looks very different for a marathon runner than for a weightlifter. Exercising regularly for a white-collar worker likely won't be the same as exercising regularly for a professional athlete. Always keep in mind that you are a unique individual. What works for me or someone else may not be as effective for you. But if you value and believe in yourself, you will make the necessary effort to come up with a curated set of sustainable good habits that work for you. Listen to your body closely and embrace the actions that yield your absolute best results. Make these actions a part of your life and you can have it both ways: a fit, healthy body and complete, utter enjoyment of your food.

Recipes

These are a few of my favorite recipes (which are always a hit at potlucks and family get-togethers) mixed in with recipes contributed by our fittest food lovers. Enjoy!

BREAKFAST/BRUNCH

Spicy Scrambled Egg Sandwich

This egg sandwich is one of my go-to breakfasts. It's packed with flavor and easy to make, especially if you make the spicy cilantro sauce ahead of time.

Ingredients:

- 2 eggs
- 2 slices of sourdough bread (or whatever your favorite hearty bread is)
- ½ avocado (thinly sliced)
- tempura sauce (I typically use Kikkoman tempura sauce)
- butter (to oil pan and butter a slice of bread)

spicy cilantro sauce a.k.a. zhoug - food processor required

- 4-5 cloves of garlic (increase or decrease the amount based on your preference for garlic)
- 2.5 cups of cilantro

- 3-4 large jalapenos (depending on your preference for spice)
- 3 tablespoons white vinegar
- ½ teaspoon of red pepper flakes
- ¾ cup extra virgin olive oil
- pink Himalayan salt or sea salt (to taste)

Directions:

1. For the spicy cilantro sauce, add all the ingredients to the food processor and process until it becomes a uniform paste and set aside.

2. Heat a pan to medium-high and coat it with a pat of butter. As the pan is heating, toast your slices of bread until they are a light golden brown to add a crispy texture to your sandwich.

3. Crack the eggs into a bowl and beat them with a fork. Once the butter is completely melted, pour the beaten eggs into the pan and scramble your eggs as you like. (I prefer to continuously scrape the eggs with a rubber spatula in a spiral motion, outside-in, as it cooks. As soon as it is solid on one side, I flip it over for a few seconds to keep it fluffy.) Remove the pan off the heat when done.

4. Butter one slice of toast, then place your scrambled eggs on top (buttered-side up). Lightly drizzle the tempura sauce on the scrambled egg. Top with sliced avocado.

5. Spread the spicy cilantro sauce on the second slice of bread and place it on the avocado and scrambled eggs to complete your sandwich.

6. Cut in half and enjoy!

LUNCH/DINNER

Bangin' Liver recommended and provided by Kelli Tennant

by Mary Shenouda, @paleochef

Ingredients:

- ⅓ cup cooking oil/fat of choice (ghee preferred)
- 1 lb chicken liver (chopped)
- 6 garlic cloves (crushed and minced)
- 1 large green bell pepper (chopped)
- 1 jalapeño (seeded and chopped)
- 1 ½ tsp to 1 tbsp cumin powder (adjust to taste)
- ½ tsp cinnamon powder
- ¼ tsp ginger powder
- ¼ tsp cloves powder

- ¼ tsp cardamom powder
- 1 lemon or lime or both (completely juiced)
- 1 tsp salt

Directions:

1. Sprinkle some salt on the chopped liver, important that the liver is chopped (especially if you don't like/are scared of liver).

2. Heat up the oil/fat in a large frying pan, keep the cover nearby.

3. Add the liver, allow the liver to brown. (1-2 minutes)

4. Once the liver has changed colors, add all the rest of the ingredients and mix well.

5. Cover and let cook for another 7-10 minutes on med-low heat.

6. When serving, be sure to scrape some of the sauce & browning in the pan for flavor.

7. Serve with an additional squeeze of lemon/lime and salt to taste.

8. Drizzle high-quality extra virgin olive oil to top it all off.

Ginisang Monggo

This hearty mung bean soup is Filipino soul food. My mom would make this for my family and me when I was living at home. It's flavorful and filling without the heavy feeling.

Ingredients:

- 1 ½ cups mung beans
- 1 tbsp garlic (diced)
- 1 pc medium-sized tomato (chopped)
- 1 medium-sized onion (chopped)
- 5 to 8 pcs medium-sized shrimp (peeled and deveined)
- 1 teaspoon shrimp paste a.k.a. bagoong (adjust according to taste)
- ⅓ cup coconut milk
- 3 cups water
- 1 teaspoon chicken broth
- ¼ teaspoon ground black pepper

Directions:

1. Put the water in a pot and bring to a boil.

2. Add the mung beans to the water and simmer until it becomes soft (about 35 to 45 minutes).

3. In a pan, sauté the garlic, onion and tomato over medium-high heat.

4. Add the chicken broth, shrimp and bagoong to the pan. Stir and cook for 2 minutes.

5. Pour the cooked mung beans. Stir and then simmer for 10 minutes.

6. Sprinkle the ground black pepper.

7. Serve hot and enjoy!

Nikki's Thai Sweet Potato Soup by Nikki Sharp (makes 3 servings for the week)

"Thai food is one of my favorite cuisines because I love all the different flavors. I once took a chef training course in Thailand, so I can confidently say that this vegan version won't fail your taste buds! If you're feeling adventurous, you can add lemongrass and a bay leaf to the stock (remove before you blend) for extra flavor and nutritional benefits." -Nikki Sharp

Ingredients:

- 1 tablespoon olive oil
- 3 cloves garlic (crushed)

- 3/4 onion (roughly chopped)
- 3-inch piece of ginger (peeled and chopped)
- 3 cans full-fat coconut milk
- 3-6 cups vegetable stock
- 6 sweet potatoes (washed and cubed)
- 1 large head of cauliflower (chopped into florets)
- 6 limes (juiced)
- 3 handfuls of cilantro (chopped)
- 1 tablespoon black pepper
- 2 tablespoons turmeric

Directions:

1. In a large pot over medium-high heat, add the olive oil, allowing it to heat until it runs quickly if you tilt the pot. Add garlic, onions and ginger to the pot and cook until the onion is translucent.

2. Add coconut milk, vegetable stock and sweet potatoes. Cover and bring to a boil. Once boiling, reduce to a simmer and cook for 5 minutes with the cover on.

3. While this is simmering, cut the green leaves off the cauliflower and chop into florets. After 5 minutes, add to your pot, along with the lime juice. Cover and allow to simmer until

the cauliflower is soft, about 5 more minutes. Add cilantro, black pepper and turmeric.

4. If using a blender, transfer and blend until smooth, otherwise use a hand blender. You can blend the mixture until fully smooth or leave it slightly chunky, whatever you prefer.

5. Divide and transfer to three serving bowls. Cover and refrigerate.

Note: A serving size is one large bowl. Add salt at this point to taste (not while making the soup). Optional to add ¼ cup black beans, quinoa, extra veggies, or ¼ cup chopped chicken.

Spicy Turkey Sausage Pasta

This pasta recipe is my go-to for pretty much any time I have to cook for a group of people. It has a lot of flavor, a little kick and is always a big hit!

Ingredients:

- 1 package of hot Italian turkey sausage (peel casing off sausages - typically in packs of 5)
- ½ cup yellow onion
- 4 cloves of garlic (chopped)

- 1/2 medium jar of julienned sun-dried tomatoes in olive oil
- 1 ½ cups sour cream
- 12 oz whole grain extra wide noodle
- ½ cup Italian flat-leaf parsley (chopped)
- ½ cup of freshly shredded Parmesan
- 4-8 shakes of red pepper flakes (add more or less to taste)

Directions:

1. Brown onion, sausage & garlic in a pan.

2. To onion, sausage & garlic; add sour cream, sun-dried tomatoes (remove from oil) and red pepper flakes.

3. Bring to a boil then turn down to medium. Simmer to thicken (~15 mins).

4. While sauce is simmering, in a separate pot, cook pasta according to box directions on the package.

5. Drain pasta, but save ½ cup of the pasta water to mix into sauce if it seems dry.

6. Serve pasta with sauce on top. Sprinkle with Parmesan and chopped parsley.

7. Enjoy!

SNACK/DESSERT

Avocado Smoothie

This smoothie is a slightly healthier version of an avocado smoothie my mom would make me as a kid. It's perfectly smooth, creamy and quite refreshing!

Ingredients:

- 1 medium avocado
- 1 ½-2 cups of almond milk (less to thicken; more to thin out)
- 1 cup of ice
- 1-2 tablespoons of manuka honey (adjust to preferred level sweetness)

Directions:

1. Blend all ingredients in a blender until smooth.

2. Pour in a tall glass and enjoy!

Glossary

Let us not allow the prophecy of the classic 2006 film *Idiocracy* to ring true. Keep our language alive!

ambrosial: extremely pleasing to taste or smell

borborygmus: sound that gas makes when moving through the intestine; stomach rumbling

carnivore: one who primarily eats red meat

concentric: type of movement that shortens a muscle

eccentric: type of movement that lengthens a muscle

ectomorph: one who is naturally lean and isn't predisposed to building muscle or storing fat

endomorph: one who is naturally stocky or curvy and is predisposed to storing fat

excitotoxins: a class of chemicals (usually amino acids, e.g. MSG and aspartame) that overstimulate neuron receptors; often found in low-calorie sodas, highly flavored snacks and processed foods

Kosher: food prepared according to Jewish dietary laws

Halal: food prepared according to Muslim dietary laws

hoity-toity: pretentious or snobbish

innocuous: harmless

macros: "macros" is short for macronutrients; the energy-giving components of food that fuel our body which include carbohydrates, protein and fat

mesomorph: one who naturally has an athletic build and is predisposed to building muscle instead of storing fat

oleaginous: oily or greasy

olfactory: relating to the sense of smell

omnivore: one who eats mostly anything

pescetarian: one who primarily eats fish and seafood

pollotarian: one who primarily eats chicken and poultry

puerile: relating to a child or childhood

saccharine: sugary

soupçon: a slight trace of flavor

vegan: one who doesn't eat any type of meat or animal products

vegetarian: one who doesn't eat any type of meat

Bonus: Whence It Began

Having written hundreds of articles about food and eating on my company's food blog, Glutto Digest, I occasionally wrote about tips on health and eating that would be beneficial to the body. This is a modified version of one of the earliest Glutto Digest articles I had written, which still holds useful information and would later inspire this book. Enjoy!

Eat Whatever You Want While Staying Healthy

Ever wonder how some people seem to eat whatever they want *and* still appear fit & healthy? Genes can play a role, but most contributing factors are completely within your control. To eat whatever you want without consequence does not exist; it will likely contribute to bad habits and poor health down the line. Whether or not genetics are on your side, in order to eat what you want and maintain good health in the long run, pay close attention to these 3 things:

1. **What goes in** — As the saying goes, "You are what you eat." So, if you want to be healthy, you should eat healthy, right? The confusing part is knowing what *eating healthy* means. First of all, unless you're an actor trying to temporarily lose weight/gain weight/attain a specific physique for a role, it may be best to avoid going on a diet. The great majority of diets exclude entire groups

of foods, which is largely unrealistic and thus temporary. Not to mention, denying yourself a world of delicious foods is no fun. Eating healthy should be a lifestyle (an *enjoyable* lifestyle at that), not just a week/month/year-long change. It is learned and practiced over time until it is second nature.

Eat in moderation. Unless you have a food allergy, or are directed by your doctor, it is not necessary to completely cut out any one type of food as it may lead to a backlash of cravings and overindulging. Eat whatever you want, but consciously savor every bite rather than mindlessly stuffing your face and overeating. According to Harvard Health Publications, "mindful eating" helps people enjoy their food more and prevents binging. Simply being aware and savoring each piece of food that enters your mouth leads to increased portion control and greater satisfaction. Maintain a healthy relationship with food as you would a personal relationship: pay attention to it, appreciate it and don't abuse it.

Minimize unhealthy foods. You might be thinking "But I thought I could eat what I want!" Yes, you can. However, eating *what* you want is different from eating *as much* as you want. Keep in mind that portions are everything. Generally speaking, the less healthy the food is, the lower the portion size should be. The following foods are Public

Enemy No. 1 due to their health-harming ingredients (trans fats, high sodium, sugars, etc.) and should be eaten sparingly:

- sugar—think "sweets, snacks and sauces": candy, desserts, sodas, fruit juices, dried & canned fruits, jams & spreads, ketchup & BBQ sauce, breakfast cereals, energy & protein bars, granola and most foods marked "light" or "low fat"
- simple carbs—think "white carbs": white bread, white rice, white pasta and baked goods (note: sugar is a simple carb as well)
- fried food—think "crispy batter coating": fried chicken, fries, chips and anything deep-fried
- salt—think "preserved and processed": canned foods, frozen foods, deli meats and condiments

Drink water. You shower/bathe with water to clean the outside of your body, so drink water to clean the inside of your body. Start ordering water instead of soda (including diet soda) or alcohol with your meals. If you miss the effervescence of soda, drink sparkling water. You can even make your own sparkling water at home. It may taste bland at first, but your taste buds with adjust over time and the flavor of your food will take center stage. If you must have flavor in your drinks, infuse your water with lemon, lime, or cucumber slices…not those water "enhancers" with sweeteners and preservatives.

You can also drink unsweetened tea or coffee as an alternative since they primarily consist of water and provide health benefits as well.

2. **How it gets in** — You use your mouth every time you eat, so it's only natural that you should pay attention to your oral hygiene. What good is a great meal if you don't have a healthy mouth to fully enjoy it? Additionally, your oral condition is a window to your overall health so you might want to take these tips seriously.

Brush at least 2x a day (once in the morning after you get up and again at night after your last meal) with a high quality electric toothbrush. Brushing twice a day with a manual toothbrush most likely isn't enough because most people don't brush long enough, or use the proper technique. It's a good idea to get an electric toothbrush that automatically turns off after you've brushed 2 minutes, sufficient time to fully brush all of your teeth. Also, while you can get about 300 brush strokes with a manual toothbrush, high quality toothbrushes can yield a mind-boggling 10,000-30,000+ brush strokes per minute.

Floss. Even the priciest top-of-the-line toothbrushes may not get in every tiny crevice between your teeth which is why it's still a good idea to floss effectively. Make it a regular habit after brushing and you'll keep your pearly white eating tools healthy over your lifetime.

3. **What goes out** — Just as what goes up must come down, what goes in must go out…for the most part. The average adult in the US consumes approximately 5.46 pounds of food a day. Most of this food makes its way through and out of your body. Otherwise, you'd end up weighing 1996.3 pounds heavier at the end of a full year! With all the food you send through your body, your digestive system needs a hand making sure everything is properly digested and ejected.

First, increase your daily intake of foods that are naturally high in fiber. These include:

- whole grains: barley, oats, birdseed, rice, rye, oat bran, nuts and raisins
- legumes: peas, soybeans and beans
- fruits: figs, prunes, apricots, dates, plums, kiwi, apples, ripened bananas, berries, pears, oranges, lemons, grapefruits and nectarines
- vegetables: broccoli, Brussels sprouts, cabbage, peppers, beets, artichokes, potatoes with skin, cucumbers, asparagus, eggplant, carrots, cassava, spinach, squash, tomatoes and rhubarb

Also, reduce your intake of these constipation-inducing foods as much as possible:

- red meat
- dairy products
- unripened bananas
- chips
- cookies
- fried foods

Not everything you eat will be eliminated because food is meant to provide your body with nourishment and energy. Enter the mighty calorie. **It's important to know that a calorie is energy. In order for your body to properly use that energy, you'll have to move it regularly (i.e. exercise daily).** According to multiple scientific studies, the most efficient form of working out is high-intensity interval training (HIIT), also known as high-intensity intermittent exercise (HIIE) or sprint interval training (SIE). This requires short bursts of all-out effort and can be completed in under 30 minutes a day…That's only 2% of your day. However, if the thought of expending maximum physical effort already stresses you out, begin with any sort of full-body movement for 30 mins each day—whether it's dancing to your favorite Pandora station, or going for a power walk around the block—to work up a good sweat and work your way up to better health. If you love food, you gotta learn to love to move.

As you incorporate these guidelines into your daily routines, they will increasingly feel like a natural part of your life. Making good eating decisions will become effortless. You will be able to eat whatever you want while staying in good health and making your relationship with food as healthy as ever.

***

Thanks for staying all the way past the "credits." Seeing that you've made it through the entire book, you likely have a good sense of what to focus on to reach your personal eating and exercise goals. If not, chances are, you skipped right to the end looking for some sort of shortcut.

Reality check: There are no shortcuts to lasting success. To understand what it takes, make sure to go through the content and absorb the valuable advice given along the way.

Don't cheat yourself. You deserve better—the best version of you.

For those of you who have read through the chapters while picking up nuggets of wisdom, I applaud you. By valuing yourself and putting in the time and effort to discover what works best for you, you're well on your way to living a healthy, happy food-filled life. CHEERS!

Made in the USA
Monee, IL
24 February 2020